Foreword by Bob Proctor

The Money Mirror

How to Connect with Your Inner Self to Create Great Sustainable Wealth

Rae Brent

Foreword by Bob Proctor

The Money Mirror

How to Connect with Your Inner Self to Create Great Sustainable Wealth

Rae Brent

Rae Brent

Lifestyle Phoenix Publishing
A Division of Lifestyle Phoenix Group Pty Ltd
PO Box 108
Albany Creek, Queensland, 4035
Australia

Admin@LifestylePhoenix.com.au

ISBN 13: 978-0-9871687-3-3

First Edition – 2010
Second Edition – 2018

Cover by: Pauline Longdon
Text by: Rae Brent

Financial Disclaimer:

This work represents the personal experience and opinions of the author and, as such, should not be taken as financial advice. The reader assumes all risk for any actions taken based upon the content or comments in this work. The author bears no responsibility for omissions or errors; the text is intended as general commentary only and is not to be considered comprehensive in any way. It is advised that each person seek competent and current financial advice from qualified professionals before investing.

Acknowledgments

*If I can see further, it is because I have stood
on the shoulders of giants*

– Sir Issac Newton

I would like to take this opportunity to acknowledge all of the *"Giants"* whose shoulders I have stood on and continue to stand on as I continue on my journey. Thank you all for allowing me to stand on your strong shoulders and learn from your experiences and wisdom.

This book is dedicated to my loving parents: Lorna Brent and Bob Brent *(deceased.)* Thank you for instilling in me the confidence to do everything that I ever dreamed of doing and supported me in my every endeavor.

To Pauline Longdon: I thank you for always being there and for supporting me to grow into the amazing woman that I have become.

To all my mentors and teachers who have shared their knowledge so freely and whose shoulders I now stand on, the view is amazing. Thank you!

To everyone who wants something more in their life and isn't afraid to go out and get it. I commend you for taking the proper action to create your reality by changing what you see in your *Money Mirror.*

Go confidently in the direction of your dreams
...Live the life you've imagined

– Thoreau

Table of Contents

Foreword by Bob Proctor 9

Introduction 11

Chapter 1: Discovering *The Money Mirror* 15

Chapter 2: Are You Seeing Clearly? 31

Chapter 3: What's Really Holding You Back? 47

Chapter 4: The Shocking Truth About Overnight Success! 75

Chapter 5: How To Take Your Financial Snapshot 95

Chapter 6: Are You Happy With What You See? 117

Chapter 7: Finding The Path To Your Perfect Life 137

Chapter 8: Making A Plan To Change Your Financial Image ... 157

Chapter 9: Discovering The Best Way To Get To Where You Want
            To Go 181

Chapter 10: Today Is The Day To Change 201

Recommended Resources 217

About The Author 219

Rae Brent

Foreword

By Bob Proctor

W hen you look in the mirror, what do you see? Are you wracked with debt, living in shambles, scrambling to make ends meet? Or do you see a confident worry-free individual, who travels the world, drives a great car, and has money to spare in your bank account?

Rae Brent is correct in that your earning potential starts with you and the way you see yourself and think about money. If you accept that your bank account is imbalanced and that you overspend, you will continue to do so and wrack up your debt. However, if you look at yourself honestly, evaluate your finances, examine your spending habits and assess your thinking relative to money, you can begin to change your relationship with money.

I made a decision long ago which allowed me to grow successfully into the person I am now – free of money worries. Money, or the lack of it, is the result of a decision you make or live by default. Rae provides some excellent questions and worksheets to help you outline what steps you need to take to get to financial and personal success.

The Money Mirror is an excellent combination of inspirational and spiritual soul food, and practical steps and planning techniques. This is no surprise, considering Rae's own background in the military, combined with her spiritual awareness.

A friend of mine, Vince Roazzi, once said, *"If you want to change your life, you've got to change your life."* It's so deceivingly simple. The decision is yours.

The Money Mirror is an excellent book for anyone wanting to improve their life or needing a reminder of how to get to the top.

Bob Proctor:

- Featured Teacher in *The Secret* and Bestselling Author of *You Were Born Rich*

Introduction

Employ your time in improving yourself by other men's writings, so that you shall come easily by what others have labored hard for

– Socrates

Wouldn't it be great to be able to stand on the shoulders of the giants who have paved the way before you? To learn from their experiences without having to go through the tough stuff yourself? I hope to share with you some of my knowledge and some I have learned from the giants whose shoulders I have stood on along my journey.

I want to empower you to look at your own way of thinking and see if it is taking you where you want to go. I can help you do this with simple exercises designed to uncover what you really want.

I call it *The Money Mirror*, and it's a way to look at your income and expenses and see them in a new light. If you don't know where you are or what you really want, how can you possibly reach your potential or end goal? *The Money Mirror* can help you see more clearly. It can spotlight beliefs or habits you have that are holding you back.

This book can help you connect with your inner self to find your path to great sustainable wealth. Notice that I said *"your"* and not *"my."* That's crucial to your success. After all, who better to define your idea of financial success than you?

I can provide you with the tools to envision and achieve financial success. I can help you let go of the beliefs that are holding you back. I've learned some things the hard way and I'd like to show you how to avoid some of the pitfalls. I've also had the opportunity to work with some incredible people and I'd like to share some of their wisdom with you too.

Don't spend another day living in financial fear. Let me show you how to use *The Money Mirror* to redirect your life and put it on the path you want to travel.

For many of us, money issues are destroying our happiness, undermining our relationships, and keeping us from achieving our goals.

If you stopped right here and now and took a good long look at your finances, what would you see? Would you be proud of your progress toward your dreams of wealth and security? Or would you be afraid of or frustrated by the mess of bills and debt?

Your past choices have brought you to this place. Where are you? Is it anywhere you want to be? Anywhere you ever thought you'd be? Or do you keep thinking that something is just not right?

The Money Mirror gives you a clear reflection of your DNA and Belief Systems (BS). If you don't like the $$ value looking back at you from *The Money Mirror*, you need to change your DNA and Beliefs (or as Bob Proctor calls them *'Paradigms.'*)

But, before you can change something within yourself, you need to identify it for what it is. Then you can acknowledge it for what it has done for you.

And when you remove negative emotions from each event you become objective. Because every event in your life has played an integral part in getting you to where you are now.

Your past beliefs, and the decisions that you have made because of them, have resulted in your current situation.

There is a definition of Insanity which basically says: *"Insanity is doing the same things over and over again and expecting a different result"*. And the same is true of your beliefs. Until you change your current beliefs, you will never move beyond where you currently are.

Be grateful for your beliefs. They now allow you to identify what is holding you back from taking *"The Next Best Step"* on your journey of personal purpose.

Take time to reflect and acknowledge all your past events that have brought you to this point in your life.

It is now time for you to *Decide* to change your beliefs, and to create great sustainable wealth in all areas of your life.

Enjoy! Your Journey starts today.

*What lies before us and what lies behind us
are small matters compared to what lies
within us... And when we bring what is within
us out into the world... miracles happen!*

– Ralph Waldo Emmerson

Chapter 1

Discovering The Money Mirror

*I believe it is my duty to make money and still
more money and to use the money I make for
the good of my fellow man according to the
dictates of my conscience*

– John D. Rockefeller

I s money destroying your happiness? Do you worry about your bills or your growing debt? Maybe you argue with your loved ones about spending or saving? Or where your financial priorities lie?

Even if your finances aren't making you miserable, they could be taking up more of your precious time than they should be. Most of us need to find jobs and earn an income. But some people never seem to be able to get ahead. They work day in and day out in jobs they don't really enjoy, just to bring home a paycheck they don't love either.

It can be difficult to know what to do with money. I've seen people spend it on the first shiny thing they see. Savings that took them months or years to accumulate are gone in an instant. Even some who are trying to save or invest, fall victim to the *"Get-Rich-Quick"* schemes. And they end up losing their hard-earned cash or even more.

Taking the First Look in The Money Mirror

This book can help you look at your finances using a tool I call *The Money Mirror*. *The Money Mirror* is simply a way to be more objective and truthful with yourself (and less emotional) about your money. When was the last time you took an honest look at your financial situation? Did you like what you saw? Chances are you're not all that thrilled.

Ask yourself questions like these:

- Is my income where I'd like for it to be? If not, where would you like it to be? Am I earning what I deserve? Is it a decent salary? What do I class as a decent salary? Am I happy with my current salary?

- Are my expenses manageable? Am I able to pay my bills in full and on time? Is my income greater than my expenses? Do I have to juggle my finances to pay my bills?

- What about my savings? Are they growing or shrinking?

- Where am I investing my money? What investment returns am I achieving? Is my wealth growing?

Now think about how the questions made you feel.

Could you answer them? Do you have a good idea of where things stand? Do you know the balances in your various accounts? What about the amounts you owe on your credit cards, home loan, and other debts? Balances on your savings account and investments? Do you know how they're growing (or even whether they're growing)?

And if you do know how your financial situation looks, were you able to decide if it is what you want? Were you left with a feeling of peace, satisfaction, or happiness? Or did the entire exercise make you unhappy or uncomfortable?

Is Money Making You Unhappy?

Money can be a source of stress and unhappiness if it's not playing its proper role in your life. Some people focus too much energy on building wealth. Sacrificing their personal happiness in the pursuit of growing account balances. While others ignore small problems until they become big problems.

These are the types of things you may begin to see in *The Money Mirror*.

If you held a mirror up to your financial self, what would you see? What would your reflection in *The Money Mirror* look like? There are many types of reflections that can signal unhappiness.

One-way money can lead to problems is by causing fear. Sometimes, these fears relate to past spending and associated accumulated debt. If you look at your financial situation, is debt the first thing you see? Are you afraid you'll never get it paid off? Do you regret past financial decisions that you did or didn't make? Future uncertainty and concern as to whether you can pay your bills is another potential fear problem.

Finances can also be a source of worry. While this is akin to fear, it may be less obvious. Money worries can take several forms. Even if you don't have problems large enough to make you fearful, money can cause you to worry. Maybe it's a matter of the day-to-day decisions of which bills to pay and which to hold onto for a few days. Or perhaps you must be very, very careful every time you use your credit card (even if it's a small amount) because there just isn't any extra in your accounts.

Financial unhappiness can also result from feeling overwhelmed by all the options. It can be very difficult to sort through the millions of potential investment opportunities and saving directions.

Every day, there are dozens of stories on the news or in the papers or magazines or on the Internet about people who have (1) made millions of dollars without a lot of effort and (2) lost millions of dollars even though they worked very hard. There are many paths you can take. But you need to find the right one for you.

Maybe frustration is your first impression when you think of money. Work, work, work to save it only to have it gone in an instant. Or maybe you are very careful in some areas of your financial life, but in other areas of your life you are out of control and these are keeping you from getting any closer to your goals. This can be very frustrating and could possibly cause problems within your relationships.

Looking at your finances can also help you see if you're letting money dominate your life too much. You may have enough to meet your needs for a home, a car, and food on the table. But do you feel satisfied?

I have a friend whose business has grown quickly in recent years. His income has grown, too, and he can now spend for luxuries. He drives a flashy car and wears better clothes. However, he doesn't seem any happier than he ever was. He can't enjoy the money, because he is so focused on earning more of it. He never has time for friends or family or nice vacations or playing golf (which he used to love.) Even so, he's planning a major expansion of his business. And although he has quite a bit of money, it's not leading him to an abundant life.

As you look in *The Money Mirror*, you may see that money is making you unhappy. You may be thinking you already KNOW money (or the lack of it) is making you unhappy. But do you know why? It may not be as simple as you think.

The Money Mirror

Have you ever been surprised by your own reflection? Not too long ago, I walked into a crowded restaurant with a group of friends. We were making our way across the room when I glanced up ahead and caught the eye of someone, and (with a jolt) I realized it was me! The restaurant had covered most of one wall with mirrors reflecting the space. It was a strange sensation to realize that the person I had made eye contact with was my own reflection.

I began to watch the mirror and the reaction of the other men and women in the restaurant. It was quite amazing! Some people caught that first glimpse and then made every effort NOT to see it again. They looked in every direction but that one. They carefully sat with their backs to the mirrors. They ducked their heads as they were leaving to avoid seeing themselves.

Of course, there were those at the other extreme who could hardly take their eyes off themselves. They watched themselves talk and smile. They adjusted their hair or their clothing.

Neither of these attitudes is particularly healthy. Why would you work so hard to avoid looking at your reflection? But it's also a little strange to ignore everything else around you to stare at yourself.

It's a lot like that with *The Money Mirror*. In the chapters to come, I'll walk you through the process of getting a good picture of your financial situation. One you can be comfortable looking at, but not too focused on. And of course, the goal is to learn how to use what you see (and what you can begin to see) to build sustainable wealth.

So, before we move on. I'd like to briefly talk about why so many of us work so hard, but never seem to get any closer to our goals.

Why Do So Many of Us Work So Hard and Never Get Ahead?

Trying to build wealth sometimes feels like running on a treadmill: you work and work and get nowhere. Reasons for this inability to get ahead can be specific things. Such as not having enough education or experience or training.

However, the specifics are only part of the issue. People with little education can make millions, and an advanced degree from a good school is no guarantee of future wealth. You don't have to look far to see evidence of this.

I have friends and acquaintances who have achieved real wealth with neither rich family backgrounds nor college educations. There are many well-known men and women who have done the same. Consider for a moment people like: Sir Richard Branson, Bill Gates, Warren Buffett and Oprah Winfrey.

The key, is that sustainable wealth is only possible if you're on the right path given YOUR innermost dreams and strengths. Sir Richard Branson, Oprah Winfrey, and Bill Gates built their wealth and power doing what they loved to do. While Oprah is clearly highly intelligent, it's hard to imagine her as a founder of Microsoft. Bill Gates is well-spoken and interesting to see interviewed, but he's not cut out to be a talk-show host or entertainer.

Each of these people who built great wealth and chances are those you know personally as well, were following their own path to success. They were working with their inner strengths, goals, and desires in areas they were and are passionate about.

Sometimes, they had to risk everything to follow their paths. But that is the choice they made and committed to follow through on. What if they hadn't stood strong in their beliefs? What if they had given up on their dreams?

Giving up would have been the most likely outcome if they had just been *"going with the flow"* or *"taking it as it comes."* They wouldn't have their wealth, but that's not the end of the story. These individuals (and many others who have built sustainable wealth) now work to make the world a better place.

While there may well be alternatives that could have led to success for Bill Gates or Oprah Winfrey. It's not impossible to see them stuck in mediocre jobs, earning mediocre salaries *if* they had not stayed true to themselves.

If you are trying to get ahead by following the advice of investment gurus or well-meaning friends or relatives. You may be dooming yourself to failure. The essential first step is to figure out where YOU want to go, and then bring together what you need to get there.

We can all think of examples of people who seemed to have all the advantages starting out in life. Maybe you have a friend with a good education or training, family connections, and intelligence who can't seem to get ahead. While these things certainly make it easier to succeed, they are no guarantee. Many highly educated people never figure out how to build their wealth (or happiness.) They may be working hard, but at the wrong things. Or they may be bouncing from idea to idea because they've never really thought through what they want to accomplish.

When you outline your goals and what financial success looks like to you. It becomes possible to take the necessary steps to get where you want to go. With a plan in place, you can discover whether further schooling would be a good idea and, if so, what kind. You can make decisions about taking a new job or quitting the one you're in with confidence that it's getting you closer to your real goals. Big purchase decisions are also easier when you know how they will affect your future.

The will to succeed is important,
but what's even more important,
is the will to prepare

– Bobby Knight

Any good plan leaves some room for updating, tweaking, or otherwise changing to meet your needs as you go through life. However, the right plan will help you stay true to the things that really matter to you. It can help you make better choices and keep you on track. It will help you decide what's important in your life, so you can be working toward what you want out of life.

There's one other thing about plans I would like to mention before we move on. I know there are some of you who have had bad experiences with *"planning."* Maybe you've come up with a plan to lose 10 kilos or save some money; perhaps it was something larger. Did it work out for you? I hope so. But if it didn't, I encourage you to think about it this way: there is a huge difference between having *"A"* plan and having the *"RIGHT"* plan for you.

One of the key purposes of this book is to help you develop the RIGHT plan for you. The right plan will be based on your own strengths (and weaknesses.) It will take you in the direction you really want to go. You'll find yourself encouraged, and it will be easier to stick with it.

Building real, sustainable wealth will be easier to achieve with your plan. And life will have more meaning and less confusion. Because you'll be able to sort through your daily decisions and see how they'll fit in with your ultimate goals.

Remember, your future is not set in stone. Through your beliefs and actions, you are constantly massaging and nurturing the direction of your future. Did you know that the Space Shuttle was off course more than it was on course when it headed towards the Moon, but it still managed to get to its end destination?

How Is Your Financial Situation Keeping You From Living The Life You Want To Live?

Simply having a lot of money is not going to guarantee you the life you want to live. My workaholic friend, for example, is certainly not happy. Rich and famous actors, rock stars, and others are often miserable. At the same time, there are those who have very little money coming in but have found deep satisfaction and a meaningful life. While their bank accounts may be small, they have found their true wealth. Think about Mother Teresa for example. She touched the lives and made a huge difference in millions of people even though she didn't have a personal fortune of money.

Therefore, it is important to understand how your finances are keeping you from the life you want to live. Just because you have lots of dollars does not mean you will be on the road to happiness.

How would you want your life to be different if you could ignore money? Is your house driving you crazy because it's too small? Do you feel unsafe in the car you drive? Would you tell your boss to get lost? Would your marriage be less stressful if you could just get out of debt?

Studies have shown that money issues are one of the big reasons marriages fail and relationships fall apart. Jay and Susan, for example, looked like the ideal newly married couple. He loved to bring her presents, many of them lavish (and expensive.) Susan was thrilled with their new home. She loved it when Jay come home with a new piece of furniture for the living room or a new cooking gadget for their kitchen.

But everything changed when she realized these sweet gestures came with a price tag that wasn't being paid. Credit card debts were piling up and bill collectors started calling. Susan felt betrayed. Jay had lied to her about the state of their finances. It'd be years before they could dig themselves out of debt (if they ever could.) And although they are trying to make a go of their marriage, arguments about money are making it very hard.

Nearly everyone would change some things in their lives if they had the ability to. So, if your financial situation is causing you problems, don't you think it's about time to change it?

If your answer is Yes, then please continue reading.

This Book Can Help

It's possible to fool yourself into believing a situation is better or worse than it is. But I want to help you get a good and true idea of your situation, as well as the underlying reasons why you are where you are.

If you don't like your current reflection in *The Money Mirror*, the next task is to decide what you do want to see. Although you might think you know the answer to that (more MONEY, of course), it's far more complicated than you might assume.

For example, are you willing to work 80 hours every week to make more money? What about 100 hours per week? How much more would it take? What is MORE money anyway? If you received $1 extra, is that technically not more money? Be more specific with what you want.

Too many times in life, we know exactly what we don't want. But when faced with the question of what we do want, we struggle to come up with anything more than vague at best.

Take some time out to reflect about what you really do want out of life. Give yourself permission to start dreaming again about what you do want in your life.

Many people have the wrong attitudes and beliefs about money. They may believe they are incapable of having high incomes or sustainable wealth. Are you one of these people? Other people, on a subconscious level, fear what will happen to them after they achieve great wealth.

When you understand what you want to see when you look in *The Money Mirror.* And you realize what thoughts and beliefs are keeping you from your vision and purpose in life. You can develop a plan for change.

So, don't wait another day. You can unlock your full potential and start to build great sustainable wealth today. This can, in turn, release you from many of the stresses you may now be facing. It can also open the door to allowing you to spend your time the way YOU want to spend it.

Whether you believe you can
or you believe you can't...
You are 100% right!

– Henry Ford

For Further Thought:

Discovering The Money Mirror

1. When you think about *"money,"* what images pop into your mind? (Examples: big houses, fast cars, piles of bills, phone calls from debt collectors, donations to charities or even the lyrics to songs about money.) Start to write them down.

    _____
    _____
    _____
    _____
    _____

2. If you had $1,000.00 in your hand right now, what would you do with it and why?

    _____
    _____
    _____
    _____
    _____

3. If you had to think of one word that best describes your feelings about your finances, what would it be?

    _____
    _____
    _____
    _____

4. How well or how poorly do these emotions fit how you feel about money?

	Not at All	Not Really	Maybe a Little	Often	VERY Much
Angry					
Frustrated					
Confused					
Afraid					
Overwhelmed					
Obsessed					
Bored					
Cheated					
Uneducated					
Out of Control					
Embarrassed					
Scared					
Betrayed					
Jealous					
Selfish					
Joyous					
Excited					
Comfortable					
Peaceful					
Proud					
Generous					

Relaxed					
Capable					
Determined					
Fascinated					
Gratitude					
Worthy					
Happy					
Satisfied					

5. Just suppose money, education and age were no barrier to you achieving all your dreams. What would Your perfect life look like? Describe it in specific detail. Imagine yourself in Your perfect life. What do you see around you? What can you hear? And how do you feel being there in Your perfect life? *(I want you to be selfish in this exercise, to the point that this is Your perfect life you are describing. Don't allow other people's opinions about what you can and can't have, be or do influence how you picture Your perfect life.)*

_____

_____

_____

_____

_____

_____

*If you don't want to write in your book... You can download all the exercises at: www.TheMoneyMirrorBook.com/resources

Rae Brent

Chapter 2

Are You Seeing Clearly?

*A problem can't be solved with the
same level of thinking that created it*

– Albert Einstein

Sometimes our emotions keep us too close to a situation that we can't see it clearly. We need to be able to remove, or distance ourselves from the situation. Then we can look at it from a different point of view.

It is said that *"beauty is in the eye of the beholder."* While I may find a certain landscape beautiful, you may find it ugly. You may love an artist's work, but I may find it disturbing.

The reason for this is, your brain interprets information based on your own personal framework. Two people can look at the same patterns and draw quite different conclusions.

Your perceptions about everything are influenced by variables such as:

- Past experiences

- Personality

- Future expectations

- Mood or state of mind

- Society's beliefs

- People around you and their perceptions, and

- Your own Belief Systems

Perceptions about your financial situation are no exception. You can't analyze money separate from who you are and where you've been. Instead, you must adjust for those things to be sure you're getting a true picture of your finances.

Let's begin to look at some of the major types of adjustments you may need to make as you look into *The Money Mirror*. Once you understand these factors, you can begin to put together a snapshot of your financial situation.

What Keeps You From Getting A True Picture?

As previously noted, many factors come into play when you attempt to ensure you get a true picture. Some are internal such as your personality or your mood or your past experiences. Others are external such as the confusing images you may get from other people whose situations you don't clearly understand.

Some are lasting and unlikely to change, such as your fundamental character traits. Others are constantly changing, such as your moods. Still others are in between, such as belief systems that you would need to make a conscious effort to alter.

It's also possible to lack the basic understanding of how to analyze your finances. A sense of self awareness is essential to get a clear picture.

No matter how well you put together the underlying information you need to assess your finances. Your emotions will affect how you interpret what you see. Your personality and past experiences shape the conclusions you draw.

Money is a very emotional issue for many people. And your emotions can keep you from seeing clearly.

Are You Fooling Yourself About Your Financial Situation?

The exercises at the end of the last chapter dealt with your money situation and what emotions it raised. You imagined your perfect life if you could ignore money. Look back through your answers.

What patterns can you see? Do your answers indicate feelings of fear? Consider how that fear might be feeding into your thoughts about money. For example, if you are afraid you won't be able to pay your bills, you may have an exaggerated sense of what you owe.

But, before we move into a step-by-step method for taking a financial snapshot. Let's look at how your *emotional self* can come into play when you look in your *Money Mirror*.

Are You Fooling Yourself About The Financial Situation Of Other People?

One of the most difficult things many people deal with when they think about money is feelings of jealousy. Looking at the spending habits of friends, acquaintances, family members, or even total strangers can lead to a deep sense of dissatisfaction and unhappiness.

Some people view their own money situation with an eye toward what they perceive other peoples' finances to be. It's so easy to fall into the trap of seeing other peoples' lifestyles and making assumptions. The problem is that it's impossible to have enough information to do this without setting yourself up for disappointment.

Cindy and John, for example, both appear to have plenty of money. They live in one of the nicest houses in one of the nicest neighborhoods. They go on lavish vacations. They drive very nice cars and have help with the lawn and the house and the childcare.

If you were to guess how much money they must be making or spending, chances are you'll be wrong. Each person or family has their own tolerance for debt.

Cindy and John may have huge credit card bills and big car loans. They may be barely making the payment on the house because of all the other amounts they owe. Or they may have scrimped and saved in the past to be able to afford to live well now.

You also don't know their current incomes or wealth. You don't know if there's some big inheritance down the road or in the past.

The bottom line is that lifestyle is not always a good indication of a person's financial situation. There are people who will maximize what they owe to make purchases. There are others who despise the idea of owing anyone anything, and who may be living well beneath their means.

It's very easy to let what you think other people are making or spending or saving affect your perceptions of your financial situation. And, your level of happiness with where you are. Both are mistakes which can influence your success. They affect your ability to take control of your money situation in a meaningful and effective way.

Past Experiences Shape Your Perceptions Of Reality

Past experiences play an important role in your view of your financial situation. Your family background and the attitudes of your parents, for example, are integral to your attitudes and beliefs toward money.

Were your parents' free spenders? If so, you may have picked up those tendencies, too. If they were very cautious with their money, there's a good chance you are, too. Sometimes, family attitudes can lead to a different mindset.

Lisa and Julie, for example, are two sisters from a working-class family. Growing up, Lisa and Julie heard many times statements like *"money doesn't grow on trees"* and *"waste not, want not."* And other expressions of their parents' deep-seated beliefs that money was something to be carefully saved in case of hard times.

The two girls found their parents' unwillingness to spend money, at times, embarrassing. Classmates made fun of the clothes that had to be worn when they were too small or tight. The family car was old and outdated. And the family rarely went out to dinner or on vacation.

Both girls had problems at times with the money mindset in the home, and each reacted to the situation in her own way.

Lisa, the elder sister, decided at an early age she would never worry about money the way her parents did. She'd make so much of it, she'd never have to think twice about going out to dinner or buying a new car. It looks like she succeeded. She now drives back into their hometown in a flashy sports car. And she tends to make big spending gestures, like highly visible donations or throwing lavish parties.

The strongest influence of her upbringing makes her want to get away from the image of a poor girl in the most visible way. She never wants to feel poor again. So, she decided she just won't worry about it. Fortunately, she has the income to make this possible (at least for now.)

Julie, on the other hand, has always been very conservative. She can't seem to enjoy spending money no matter how much she has. No savings account is ever big enough for Julie. And she tends to assume the worst will happen as far as finances go. She remembers all the times her parents mentioned costs and those attitudes are deeply ingrained.

Neither Lisa nor Julie would be likely to see clearly if they looked in their *Money Mirror*. Lisa might be haunted by the images of the little poor girl in the worn-out clothes. And Julie would tend to see things darker than they are. While Lisa might see her spending as part of what makes her happy, Julie wouldn't feel the same way.

To get to a true reflection and a good idea of what they really want, both would need to look in *The Money Mirror* while fully aware of their past experiences. They need to understand that their emotions about money can influence how they see their finances. Their emotions can also play a role in their thoughts about the future. Without first considering the past experiences influencing your thoughts about money, you can't hope to see your financial picture clearly.

Your Personality Affects Your Perceptions About Money

Another consideration is your personality. And whether it tends toward optimism or pessimism. While other components of character also partly determine your perceptions about money, the *optimism-pessimism* variable is one of the most important. It can also affect the kinds of things you attract into your life.

Do you tend to look on the bright side? Do you see the glass as half full? Do you think your ship is going to come in, and soon? Maybe you tend to take a more negative view. Either way, your view of your money situation will be affected, particularly when you try to make predictions about the future.

An optimistic-pessimistic point of view affects several aspects of your financial snapshot:

- Values you place on things you own (such as your house, your car, and other assets) are partly determined by your personality. If you tend to be overly optimistic, for example, you might assume you could sell those things for more than you realistically could

- The amounts of insurance and savings for a rainy day you feel are necessary can also be influenced by your perspective

- Projections about future earnings, expenses, and other items are clearly driven by your point of view

It is appropriate for your plan to reflect your personality. But make sure it is realistic. If you are a *"worrier"* who tends to be concerned that bad things might happen in the future, planning to protect yourself with extra savings might be one adjustment. However, it would be impossible to reach your financial potential if you were unrealistically grim about every assumption and decision.

I have some friends who tend to over think the negatives in their financial decisions. Every time they are presented with a decision, they start with lists of pros and cons and spreadsheets.

They think about the things that might happen and many others that are so unlikely as to be ludicrous. By the time they're through, they've come up with dozens of bad thoughts, downsides and reasons not to move forward.

If they must make a guess about the future, they always take the negative view (they won't get raises, their cost of living will go up wildly, they might lose a job, they might get sick.)

Not only is this a real waste of their energy, it also leads them to make bad decisions sometimes. By the time they finish putting on the potential negatives, they can't make an objective decision. They are always very conservative, and they don't enjoy the money they do spend.

If they would just understand this tendency, they could at least begin to adjust for it in their planning. If they could see more clearly, they would be empowered to make better choices and live the life they want to live.

Being too positive can also be a problem. If you always think your income is going to rise unrealistically fast and your expenses will be unrealistically low, you might find your plan getting you nowhere. You might even go backward.

So how do you know if you're too far to one end of the spectrum or the other?

Did your answers to the exercises at the end of the last chapter tend to be strongly emotional? If you strongly agreed that money made you feel overwhelmed, embarrassed, cheated, obsessive, afraid, annoyed, scared, and other negative emotional words, you may tend to see your financial situation more negatively than is justified.

We all tend to know whether we are usually optimistic or pessimistic (though this can change with circumstances.) The ability to identify when you may be going too far in one direction or the other is important to seeing clearly in your *Money Mirror.*

Being "In Denial"

Some people even tend to deny the existence of problems. They shut down and simply choose not to see what they don't want to see. Being *"in denial"* can apply to any bad situation in your life from relationships to health to work and beyond. While it can be an important coping mechanism, it certainly affects the ability to see clearly.

If you have a financial problem you don't admit to yourself and deal with, chances are it will grow worse. This is not contrary to the notion that we need to choose to think positive thoughts to attract good things into our lives. Instead, the idea is to fully admit problems to yourself to begin to make real change.

How Did You Get Where You Are Today?

Another factor shaping your ability to see clearly is the financial path you've been traveling. Some of you are moving in very clear financial directions. This is particularly true when you're young. It may be easy to see all your income and expenses and assets and debts. It may be as simple as looking at the balance and flows through one account. However, if you have been investing for a while, chances are you're going to have to work through a lot of complexity to get to a clear picture.

The path you've been on also influences your perceptions, as described above. If you've just been through a rough patch, you may have to take that into consideration when you look in *The Money Mirror* today.

Your Current Mood

How you got to where you are today can shape your mood. Other things can also affect your mood. By mood, I mean anything that changes your perspective or outlook on life in a temporary way. Mood is related to personality, and the same issues of optimism and pessimism can come into play.

However, mood can also stem from more transitory factors ranging from the weather to the traffic to whether you had an argument with someone at your office.

It is important to account for mood when you look in *The Money Mirror*. If you're in a great state of mind, you may tend to see things too brightly. If you're feeling low, you may view them darkly.

Mood is yet another example of how we can let our emotions dictate our perceptions when we look in *The Money Mirror*. You may want to spend a few minutes considering things going on in your daily life that could change the way you think about money. It's a bad idea to base long-term plans on conditions that only apply to today.

If you are in a great mood because your favorite sports team won a major game, wonderful! If you are you in a bad mood because you were caught in traffic and late for work? Understandable! However, these kinds of things really have nothing to do with your *Money Mirror.*

Whenever I'm facing a big financial decision, I think about my general state of mood. If it's particularly good or bad right then, it's important to be aware of that fact. Sometimes, I make a preliminary decision and then come back to it in a couple of days to be sure I still feel it's the right one. That way, if I've been overly influenced by the emotion of a moment, I can recognize and adjust if needed.

Your Expectations For The Future

Although I talk of looking in *The Money Mirror* and taking a financial snapshot, it is impossible to stop time to conduct the analysis. You can't ignore the past and where you came from (though you can work to change it), you also can't neglect your thoughts about the future.

Any financial picture must be a snapshot in time. Chances are you can't be consistently on top of:

- Precise balances on all accounts

- Exact values of all assets

- To-the-cent totals of outstanding debts

Moreover, you can't possibly know what the future will bring. It's certainly possible (and desirable) to get a general feel for likely future directions. But it's impossible to know with certainty.

Uncertainty about the future can affect your ability to see the current patterns clearly. It can also lead you to tend to see positives or negatives more strongly. Future expectations can be tied to your tendencies toward optimism or pessimism, of course, but they can also exert their own influence.

Are You Seeing Your Image Clearly?

Money can be a source of stress and unhappiness if it's not playing its proper role in your life.

Some people focus too much energy on building wealth, sacrificing their personal happiness in the pursuit of growing account balances. While others ignore small problems until they become big problems.

These are some of the things you'll begin to see in *The Money Mirror*.

If you held a mirror up to your financial self, what would you see? What would your reflection in *The Money Mirror* look like?

If you don't get a clear picture of where you are, it's extremely difficult to build the best plan moving forward.

By looking at your state of mind, personality, past experiences, and other characteristics, you can begin to see how your financial image of yourself might be distorted.

Sometimes, these conditions need to change to allow you to achieve wealth. For example, if you're overly pessimistic, your negative view might make you pass up some good opportunities and keep you from finding your best path to the life you want.

At other times, however, all that's required is a simple awareness and a commitment to make the necessary changes. If you know you tend to look to the dark side, for example, you can compensate as needed when you look in *The Money Mirror*.

Each of us has a unique attitude toward money shaped by many factors. Understanding these underlying tendencies can help you begin to see more clearly.

For Further Thought:

Are You Seeing Clearly?

1. What was the prevailing attitude about money in your home when you were a child? What are some of your earliest money memories? What were your parent's favorite sayings about money?

    _____

    _____

    _____

    _____

    _____

    _____

    _____

2. How do you think those early memories and emotions affect your perceptions about money today? Were they positive memories? Negative? Do they affect how you view money now?

    _____

    _____

    _____

    _____

    _____

    _____

3. Would you describe yourself as an optimist or a pessimist?

    _____

    _____

4. Do you think other people would describe you the same way? Your family? Co-workers? Acquaintances? If not, why not?

    _____
    _____
    _____
    _____
    _____
    _____

5. Think of times when you've had to make assumptions about whether (a) something good or (b) something bad would happen. Do you tend to expect good things?

    _____
    _____
    _____
    _____
    _____
    _____

6. Consider all the many things affecting your current mood. Think of a time when you were in an exceptionally great mood or bad mood. How might your mood affect your ability to see clearly if you looked in *The Money Mirror*?

    _____
    _____
    _____
    _____
    _____
    _____
    _____

7. Do you tend to deny the existence of problems, choosing not to see the bad situations in your life? When did this start?

_____

_____

_____

_____

_____

_____

_____

8. If you do go into "denial" about issues, how do you think this affects your financial situation?

_____

_____

_____

_____

_____

_____

_____

If you can't be honest about your money situation with anyone else … at least be honest with yourself.

Why? Because you are only hurting yourself if you don't. And you could be making things worse by not identifying patterns early on when there's still a chance to correct your current direction.

*If you don't want to write in your book… You can download all the exercises at: www.TheMoneyMirrorBook.com/resources

Chapter 3

What's Really Holding You Back?

A Quick Note On Limiting Beliefs:

Before we move forward, I want to very briefly introduce you to limiting beliefs. Limiting beliefs are beliefs you have about yourself that can keep you from achieving your full potential. They can shape your actions in such ways that they exert real power over you and your success in life.

For example, if you believe you aren't capable of being creative, you probably won't free your mind to let creative energy flow. Your belief that you aren't creative stifles your creativity.

Limiting beliefs and their power over you and your actions are very important, and as such, I wanted to mention the idea to make you aware of the role these limiting beliefs can play.

As you work to decide where you want to go in your financial life, identify the negative or limiting thoughts that enter your head - make a list as you go. The sky is not the limit here; think in terms of where you really want to go NOT in terms of where you think you can go.

Once you have identified negative or limiting beliefs, it is an easy process to learn to replace them with empowering beliefs using different techniques.

We are not limited by our imagination...
We are only limited by our belief systems!

– Pauline Longdon

What's Holding You Back

What do you think is the single biggest hurdle between you and your perfect life? The straightforward, but potentially surprising, answer may be yourself and your self-limiting beliefs.

Many of us have never really thought about these internal systems of deeply held beliefs, yet they color our perceptions, our thought processes, and our decisions.

You may be saying to yourself: *What? My self-limiting beliefs? What in the heck are those? I do have beliefs, but I would never have self-limiting beliefs ...I've seen the movie "The Secret."*

What are your self-limiting beliefs? Where do they originate? It's important to identify your self-limiting beliefs and take action to rid yourself of them if they stand between you and your perfect life?

When you consider the questions and thoughts that inform your decision-making process, you will begin to see that the process is circular. You can think about your belief systems from front to back, or back to front. You would never consciously make decisions that would keep you from reaching your goals, but your deeply held beliefs may be bringing about that result.

Exploring Self-Limiting Beliefs

Self-limiting beliefs can be defined as those long-held, ingrained ideas that are imbedded in your psyche which set up roadblocks in your thought processes. And they keep you from attaining your goals and dreams.

To move forward in your quest for financial freedom and wealth, you must examine and sweep out any negative beliefs that are blocks on your road toward your goals. This is a little bit like cleaning house. You must clean out the cobwebs in your belief systems; they are limiting the growth of new and better ideas and beliefs.

In other words, let go of beliefs that set you up for failure and instead open yourself up to all possibilities. Remember, self-limiting beliefs only exist in YOUR mind.

While self-limiting beliefs can be very personal, there are several types that tend to affect many of us. The following sections describe some self-limiting beliefs that have held many back from realizing their dreams, achieving financial security, and attaining wealth.

1. Beliefs Formed In Childhood

The mind is a powerful instrument. It can positively or negatively impact your ability to reach your goals. Your mindset, attitudes, and beliefs directly influence your actions toward the realization of your dreams.

Many of these beliefs were set during your childhood, during the Imprint period 0 – 7 years. It's been said *"what you are is where you were when."* And that critical age is ten years old according to some experts. So, where were you? And what was happening in your life at age 10?

It's further been stated, those beliefs set at age ten will not change unless you experience a major, traumatic, mind-changing event. Or, unless you make a conscious effort to alter them.

So, if your family struggled financially, your attitude toward money would probably be that you should save every dime you could, work hard, avoid all risks, and be content to have a secure job that provided a *"good"* income.

A good example of the impact of childhood experiences on the development of beliefs is the entire generation of Americans (and, in fact, people worldwide) who were shaped by *The Great Depression* of the late 1920s and early 1930s.

In October of 1929, the American Stock Market crashed. Literally overnight, many people lost everything they had! And by 1932, at least 12 million people were out of work in the US alone. That was one-fourth of all those who would normally work.

The Depression went on and on and impacted every facet of American life. People lost their homes, their farms, and all means to support themselves. Shanty towns made up of cardboard houses and campfires sprung up all over America.

For those who were 10 years old during this time, when their family had been rich or at least comfortable before that fateful day in October 1929. Their family's loss of money, security and the experience of abject poverty became a major, traumatic, life-changing experience.

Thus, when these children became adults, their attitudes toward money had already been shaped by these early experiences. Many of them became the first conservationists or recyclers because they believed the adage *"waste not, want not."*

In some families, these frugal patterns included actions such as clipping coupons and saving the buttons off old blouses or shirts before using them for rags. Nothing was thrown away or given to a charity; instead it was reworked into quilts or other clothing. Indeed, clothing was sometimes made from old flour sacks.

So, after observing these things as children (age ten), although they were quality attributes, they became self-limiting beliefs for these children when they became adults. Particularly as far as their financial goals or dreams were concerned.

These children of the Depression, in turn, passed on many of these attitudes to their own sons and daughters. Many opted for safe and secure. Never daring to dream a dream or take a risk that might have brought more financial security or more personal satisfaction and happiness. They became the epitome of the *"work ethic."*

2. Acquisition Of Things

Another self-limiting belief that is particularly common is that *"the acquisition of things is a very worthy goal and is a source of happiness."* The generation known as *"Baby Boomers"* provides another great example.

Following World War II, when women had joined the work force, the acquisition of things became the overpowering goal of many. After all, there was going to be a *"chicken in every pot and a car in every garage"* according to the political mood of the time.

There were many new products, and the acquisition of them became all important. Referring to beliefs formed in childhood, it would only follow that when the ten-year olds of this era became adults, their idea of success would be based on the things they acquired.

For these people, the size of the house they lived in, the car(s) they drove and the country club they belonged to enhanced their image as a success.

These parents lavished their children with their own television sets, their own phones, their own cars, and the cycle of acquisition of things went on.

They did not think about tomorrow because the *"good times would always roll on,"* and after all, they had to keep up or outdo everyone in their social circle. They believed they deserved everything.

If something breaks, throw it away and buy a new one. If a new gadget comes out, be the first to own it. Even if it means standing in line all night long. Everything is instant and easy gratification. ATMs dispense cash anytime day or night and easy credit is available via credit cards. Credit cards were often maxed out even though both parents worked.

So, why is the belief in the acquisition of things a self-limiting belief? The answer is because these things don't bring true happiness. And those who follow this path become *"slaves to the rat race"* and never stop to evaluate where they are or where they want to go. They don't have a dream and make a plan to reach that dream.

There is a tremendous amount of pressure placed on parents today to buy things. A lot of things, for their children. The source of this pressure is partially the influence of peer pressure by their children.

If you are a parent, how many times have you heard *"but everyone has one"* from your child? How many times, no matter how hard you tried to resist, have you succumbed to that pressure?

In some cases, parents' feelings of guilt, stemming from spending insufficient time with their children (due to work or other commitments), lead to a tendency to purchase things to make up for this lack (or perceived lack.)

Ask yourself… How many…

- $100 brand name shirts have I bought?

- $200 pairs of athletic shoes have I bought?

- $400 video game systems have I bought?

- $60 games for those game systems have I bought?

- Music systems have I bought?

- Television sets have I bought?

- Mobile phones have I bought?

- $50,000 cars have I bought?

Now ask yourself, where are all these *"have-to-have"* things today?

Do you still have them? Did you sell them in a garage sale? Did you throw them away? How long did they last until a newer, better, or more expensive version came out that you just had to have? Did they bring you happiness? Did they bring your children happiness?

Add up the money spent. Did the purchase of those things help or hinder you in the attainment of your goal toward real wealth and real happiness for you and your family?

3. Beliefs Imposed By Others

It's also been said, *"you are a part of all you've seen."* The person you are today is a reflection of the cumulative effect of all you've encountered throughout your life.

And the building of your self-identity certainly begins in childhood. The accumulation of any negative projections by others toward you usually develops a self-limiting picture of yourself.

Parents, often unknowingly, are guilty of this by lauding the accomplishments of one sibling over another. The message received is that you are just not as smart, gifted, or athletically talented as your brother or sister.

Another pitfall parents who want their children to *"always do their best"* fall into is adding a *"but"* to any praise bestowed on their children:

- That's a great paper, *but you should have....*

- You played a great game, *but you should have....*

Over time the message received is, *"I'm not good enough and I'll never please them, so why try?"*

Jim was a young man who was born with great potential. He was very precocious. From infancy his rapid development was often commented upon. He walked, talked, and formulated sentences at a very young age. He was a happy young man who always wanted to please his parents.

In school, he excelled in academics and sports. His parents, who were both accomplished, however, demanded perfection. They often criticized or questioned the slightest miscue.

As time went on and the advanced classes became more challenging and sports became more competitive, he felt there was no way he could meet his parents' expectation.

He decided just to *"drop out"* and began hanging out with the wrong crowd. He got into drugs. He quit the athletic teams. He took the easier classes. Finally, he dropped out of high school. His parents wondered what they had done wrong. Why had such a promising young man gone so awry?

Students in school today often receive conflicting messages. The big red X across a writing assignment or the Xs on every math problem send the message *"I taught you, but you were just too dumb to get it."*

What students don't realize is that teaching, and learning is a two-way street. And the teacher who wrote the Xs was also grading him or herself on their inability to teach so the student could understand. Hence, the self-limiting belief of *"I'm not good in school"* becomes imbedded in that child's mind.

The flip-side of that example is when students receive undeserved praise and rewards for very little effort on their part. The teacher may know the work doesn't reflect what the student is capable of producing. Or they may know they haven't presented challenging lessons.

The result is students get mostly A's, and that looks good for the teacher. However, for the students, the message received is *"I can do just enough to get by, and I'll still be alright."*

Julie, for example, was a bright student. She didn't work hard in school because she didn't have to in order to make excellent grades.

But the very first academic challenge she faced was when she went away to college. She was very bright; she knew her abilities. Julie was also very perceptive. She felt some animosity toward those high school teachers. She questioned even more the educational institutions that would allow their students not to be challenged that would; in fact, waste the precious commodity of time, time you can never get back.

The attitudes and actions that ensue become habits which, in turn, become self-limiting beliefs. Other things occur in schools that may become self-limiting beliefs about ones' self.

4. Relationships

Another area that makes one vulnerable to self-limiting beliefs is in the arena of personal relationships. This may be on the job, in social interactions, or in marriage.

In a work setting, you may find yourself subject to a domineering, hyper-critical boss, petty jealousies, and unhealthy competitions. You may be subjected to people who are immature in their interaction with others. In these situations, as an adult, you must see these for what they are. And either, not let them affect you or remove yourself from the situation.

Probably, as adults, the most perilous situation where self-limiting beliefs can take hold is in your relationship with your marriage partner or significant other. All too often, because of the closeness of the relationship, one partner may feel perfectly comfortable saying things to the other that he or she would never say to anyone else.

For example, it is often the insidious daily comments about the *"small"* things that take root and develop into self-limiting beliefs.

Have you ever heard the following?

- You're too fat.

- That was a lousy meal.

- This house is a disaster!

- Where are my clean shirts?

- Why didn't you do …?

- Where did you spend all the money?

- I don't want you to get mad, I'm just telling you this for your own good.

Over time, these comments add up. And BINGO! You are right down there on the bottom, questioning your self-worth and believing you are not capable of doing anything right.

5. The Allure Of The Media

We have all heard the question, *"Has anyone heard any good news today?"* If you spend much time watching television or reading newspapers or news journals, you would surely wonder if anything good ever happens.

Apparently, bad news sells. In today's economic climate, the question would surely be apt. If you listen long enough to the economic prognosticators or *"talking heads,"* you would likely be led to believe the future is bleak and all is doom and gloom.

This might cause you to believe that you, with your knowledge and resources, should certainly not take any financial risks. As has been noted previously, there are many negative and depraved actions taking place in our society today.

Corporate scandals can rock stock markets and send values of shares plunging instantly. Of course, the media is right there to document every sordid moment and deliver it right into your home.

Listening to negative news reports; reading negative newspapers, magazines, and books; and listening to negative music can have a very detrimental effect on your thoughts and actions. It can cause you to have a negative attitude and ultimately reduce your chances of reaching your goals.

6. Past Experiences, Failures, And Excuses

Past bad experiences and failures may lead to excuses for not taking positive action toward your dream of success and wealth. Maybe your life experiences have caused you to become a skeptic about any new venture. Your immediate response when a new opportunity is presented to you may be to declare that it won't work.

Some people have experienced failure through bankruptcy and are afraid to try again. If you are in the workforce rat race of juggling work, home, and children, you may put off making changes by saying that you don't have time right now. You might also say the same thing about going back to school to acquire new skills. What you are really saying is *"I don't believe in myself enough to take the necessary steps."*

Actions You Can Take

This discussion of common self-limiting beliefs can be used as a backdrop for you to begin to examine your own belief systems and consider how they may be affecting your ability to build and sustain wealth. Some of the areas discussed may apply to you, and some may not. Once you begin to understand the types of things that can be causing problems, you can identify the beliefs you hold that are keeping you from achieving your dreams and ultimate wealth.

In each of the six areas discussed, there are things you can do to change them.

1. Beliefs Formed In Childhood

For those beliefs instilled as a child, you as an adult can recognize them for what they are and determine not to accept them as your "*modus operandi.*"

Get out a picture of yourself when you were ten years old and take a good look at yourself. Were you brave, happy, positive, confident, and excited about the future? Did you believe then that you could tackle just about anything and accomplish it? If you were that person at age ten, what caused you to change?

Sally, for example, became very successful in her profession, says that she would always look at what other people were doing and think *"I can do that, and I can do that better."*

She was an excellent and inspiring teacher at age 35. She had two children, work and home responsibilities, but she had always wanted to do more in her profession.

Although she had many reasons not to go back to school, she earned an advanced degree and several additional certifications. And with the help and support of her family, she did this in just two and a half years while still teaching, taking care of her children, and moving into a new home.

She became a supervisor and a principal. She helped bring about many important changes in her school district. Her influence and leadership had a very positive impact not only on the community, but on the lives of the students and teachers in the school where she was principal.

Did your parents articulate ideas about the future such as educational expectations? Look at that picture, think back, and really analyze the messages you were receiving.

Were the adults in your life fearful and wary of new ventures and afraid to take risk? If you were observing these things, the belief you were internalizing was *"I'd better play it safe because you never know what (bad things) might happen."*

Looking back and analyzing the roots of your self-limiting beliefs could just be the traumatic, life-changing event in your life where you consciously do everything in your power to get them out of your belief system.

2. Acquisition Of Things

To get out of the acquisition of things and the rat race, you can choose to re-evaluate your priorities and take appropriate action. Think about what is really important to you. Think about who you really are inside and what really brings you true happiness and satisfaction.

Is the image you have of yourself more important to you than the image you want others to have of you? Are you being true to yourself?

These types of issues are at the heart of overspending, which can make you feel you are in so far over your head financially that you can't see the light at the end of the tunnel. There are things you can do to work to control your acquisition-oriented mentality.

Analyze your purchases. Are they want-to-haves or need-to-haves? If they are need-to-haves, such as a car, does it need to be the biggest or most expensive to meet the needs of your family? Before you go shopping, make a list, know where to go, and purchase only those things on your list.

Do not give in to impulse spending. If you don't just go looking, there are many unnecessary purchases you will not make. Always remember these impulse purchases may bring short-term happiness, but they certainly will not bring long-term happiness because there is always a newer and flashier possibility just around the corner.

If you are one whose parents lavished you with *"everything,"* ask yourself if those things made them or you happy. Was the time spent doing simple things together as a family the most satisfying and enduring? Chances are, your favorite childhood memories revolved around time spent together rather than things received.

It can be difficult to look deep within yourself to see your real feelings, but the acquisition of things rarely brings true joy and happiness. You can break the cycle, not pass those habits on to your children, spend a lot less, and get out of the rat race of *"keeping up appearances."* Make that connection with your inner self and determine what you really value.

3. Beliefs Imposed By Others

For those self-limiting beliefs imposed on you by others, remember you, and only you are in control of your thoughts and how you feel about yourself and what you can accomplish. Again, you will have to really think about the past experiences in your formative years that caused those self-limiting beliefs about yourself to take root.

It is a given that the largest percentage of your waking hours during your formative years were spent in a school setting or activities surrounding school. Think about your own experiences during that time. First identify the negative messages you received, really think about them and why you were the recipient of such messages.

Maybe the sender was not aware of the message being sent to you. Your parents or teachers surely would not consciously want to do anything that would hurt you. Perhaps they were doing what they did in the only way they knew how because of the way they had been raised or taught.

The bottom line is that once you identify the sources of and reasons for those *"I'm not good enough and I'm not smart enough"* negative beliefs, you can replace them with *"I AM good enough and I AM smart enough to accomplish anything I choose"* thoughts. Believe in yourself and think only positive things about yourself and you may be amazed at the difference it makes.

4. Relationships

For those beliefs imposed on you by others, remember you are in control of how you let those negative words affect you. In relationships, you can choose to turn those negative beliefs into positives by helping those you are in contact with daily see the results of positive thoughts and actions.

It is true you can remove yourself from these relationships. However, that may not be an action you, for your own reasons, are willing to take. You can recognize these relationships for what they are and refuse to let them affect you because you know who you are.

If you choose to change the relationship, particularly with your spouse or significant other, there is something you can do. Remember they may not realize the negative impact they are having on you and your feelings about yourself. They surely wouldn't want to hurt the one they love. So, the next time a negative comment comes your way. Be specific and tell the person exactly how that comment makes you feel.

5. The Allure Of The Media

Where the media is concerned, you can choose to simply pull the plug on all the negativity. Indeed, why would you want to continually let this negative drivel and garbage fill your mind?

How many times do you have to hear those negative sound bites until they enter your belief system as the truth? How many times do you have to see or hear those degrading images until they enter your belief system as *"normal"* and okay to hold?

It doesn't take very long until you have allowed the media to undermine your belief system. The result is you may be blinded to opportunities that will bring you success, wealth, happiness, and fulfillment. The immortal words of James Allen, *"As a man thinketh in his heart, so is he"* has never been truer. Just say no to the allure of the media!

6. Past Experiences, Failures, And Excuses

With past bad experiences, refuse to let them entrap you. If you are alive, which you obviously are, there is always a way. Many wealthy people have experienced bankruptcy and found the courage to begin again and become even wealthier.

Many people have analyzed the rat race they were in and decided to get out. Others have found the time to go back to school to acquire new skills, many when they were older.

Fear should not limit you! Debts should not limit you! Lack of training should not limit you! Age should not limit you!

If you procrastinate and do not make a plan and work the plan, where will you be one year from now? Five years? Ten years? You will be in the same place you are today, only older.

Live your life so that when you look back, you have no regrets about what you did or didn't do. Be forward looking... Take action... No excuses!

Decide – Commit – Act!

The above may sound oversimplified. Like you can just wave a magic wand, and all those self-limiting beliefs will simply go away.

The truth is, you'll need help and support. You can attend motivational seminars, read positive, forward-looking books, and surround yourself with forward-looking people. You can find a mentor who believes in you and helps you believe in yourself.

A teacher of young children used a song with her students before any new venture was undertaken. The song simply said, *"I think that I will try; I think that I can do it; I think that I will try; for I know that I can do it."*

Through the years, this teacher heard back from former students and their parents. One student, in his application to a prestigious university, wrote that this teacher had positively influenced his life more than any other teacher.

Another example of the positive results of having a mentor is that of a young man from a very poor family who lived in a ghetto in a large US city. He was recruited to play basketball for a small university hundreds of miles away.

He could hardly read and was ill-prepared for academic endeavors, but a kind and caring woman whose son was already on the team took him into her home, made him feel like family, and helped him improve his reading and other skills. He went on to graduate, played professional basketball, and became the coach of a professional basketball team.

If you are selective in your choices, you can find music, movies, and books filled with can-do messages. Affirmations and positive themes can easily be changed into positive beliefs.

A positive approach can be an important first step to changing your belief systems. By surrounding yourself with encouraging messages, ideas, and thoughts, you can set the stage for dealing with the problem areas.

As noted, these self-limiting beliefs are common and affect many people. However, each of us has our own specific paradigms which drive our belief systems.

What Informs Your Decision-Making Process?

As previously stated, though common, these beliefs may or may not apply to you. It is essential for you to identify for yourself what self-limiting beliefs you hold. You must really connect with your inner self, not just think superficially, and identify those self-limiting beliefs that inform your decision-making process.

We all live in a very busy world. From the time we get up in the morning until we lie down at night, many of us rush from our home, to school, to work, to sports practices or events, the doctor or dentist, to shopping for our family. When we finally get home at night, there is still homework to be completed, dinner to be prepared, laundry to be done, or tending to the needs of another family member or friend.

When we stop at the end of the day, the first thought on our minds is that we need to relax and get a little rest before we do the same thing all over the next day. When we finally get to bed, we are making a mental list of things that must be done tomorrow. Instead, ask yourself…

- Why did I do the things I did today?

- Could I have simplified them?

- Did I help someone today?

- Did I stop and really listen to my children, my spouse, my friends, and others important to me?

- Did I really have meaningful conversations with my family?

- Did I make a difference in someone else's life today?

Since many of us rarely have time to think about much of anything beyond our to-do lists some days, it is hardly surprising that we don't examine the underlying problem paradigms holding us into our damaging behavior patterns.

Your long-held, deeply rooted self-limiting beliefs do exert an extremely powerful force on your habits and your decision-making processes.

Think about this statement you have heard many times: *"If we do not study the past, we are doomed to repeat it."* Examine this statement considering your present decision-making process.

It's time for you to take stock. Here are some questions you might ask yourself while you're doing this self-examination:

1. Are you subject to advertising come-ons? For example, suppose you can get 55% off the price of new products if you spend $350.00. It sounds like a good deal. However, isn't the first decision whether you need the products or want the products? Is the company's purpose to help you, or is it to increase its bottom line by increasing sales through impulse spending on your part? Marketing can be very sophisticated, specialized, and tailored to reach a particular audience. It can be a powerful force to resist since it is often targeted and well designed.

2. Do you have a need for the approval of others? Do you find yourself considering others' reactions before you make a decision? While it's certainly appropriate to think about the way our actions affect others, it can be debilitating if taken to an extreme. Nancy once stated that she could not make any decision until she had looked at it through the lenses of what her mother would do or think. If you find yourself constantly looking for approval from others rather than making decisions from your own strengths, you are unlikely to be able to make real progress toward your goals.

3. Is your thinking short term or long term? Do you know there are long-term considerations you should be thinking about today, but you keep putting them off until tomorrow and tomorrow and tomorrow? Do you put buying a new

car every year ahead of saving toward your children's college, hoping they will earn a scholarship? Do you avoid thinking about what you will do when you reach retirement and do nothing until suddenly that time has arrived, and you are not prepared? An ad on television advertising long-term financial planning stated that *"fifty is the new forty"* meaning that as life spans (including working life spans) grow longer, we have more time for living (and, hence, a greater need for financial planning.) You don't need a nip and a tuck; you need a plan.

4. Is your thinking based on keeping others happy? Do you just go along to get along? Do you buy things for others to please them or to please yourself? Again, this can be a very positive attribute, but it can also lead to destructive behaviors such as overspending. Analyze your spending *"triggers"* to see what types of events or emotions lead to your purchases. Is it a real (or even a perceived) need for the item or is it something else? Is your thinking based on your definition of success? Is it more important to have cash in your pocket or money in your savings account? Are outside appearances more important to you than inner peace, happiness, and contentment?

5. Are you an enabler? Do you allow or even encourage others to be dependent on you because of your own needs, even though it is not in your best interest (or theirs)? Are you really helping them? Are you really helping you? Are you allowing people to energetically connect to you and have a negative influence on your energy levels?

6. Do you think other people owe you? If so, why? Do you think your boss owes you a big salary, long vacations,

health care, retirement plan, and other perks? Do you think your parents owe you a large inheritance and help any time you are in a bad spot? Do you think your children owe you just because you raised them and paid for their college education? Do you think the government owes you a fully-funded retirement, free health care, or a free education?

As uncomfortable as the realization may be, however, no one owes you anything. There is no such thing as a *"free lunch."* Someone must pay for everything.

Remember there is real satisfaction and sense of accomplishment when you do things for yourself. Waiting for others to do things for you (and feeling entitled) can keep you from taking steps toward your goals.

Examine A Recent Decision

One way to identify self-limiting beliefs is to think about a recent decision about something important to you that you made. And re-examine it in light of your awareness of the potential for problematic belief systems.

For instance, have you recently had to make a decision about a better job or other opportunity and whether you would try to attain it? Major purchase decisions (such as for a new home or car) can also be informative.

- What was your first reaction when you heard about the new job or when the idea of the purchase initially occurred to you? Was it positive (such as excitement or happiness) or negative (such as a lack of confidence or guilt)?

- What did you consider in your decision? Was it something like the self-limiting beliefs previously described? For example, did you feel you should avoid the opportunity or purchase because of the negative things you've been hearing on the news?

- Rethink the decision making a conscious effort to avoid the self-limiting thoughts you may have engaged in previously.

- Would you have reached the same conclusion?

After you've been truly introspective and completed the above exercises. You're ready to make a plan to attack your self-limiting beliefs and implement it.

Once you eliminate your self-limiting thoughts and actions. And you truly BELIEVE you can reach your goal of acquiring sustainable wealth. You'll be ready to begin your journey.

Remember that your self-limiting beliefs create an impediment to reaching your goals and realizing your dreams. Inaction, procrastination, and poor self-image are devastating and must not be accepted or used as excuses. Being motivated toward action is imperative, and self-limiting beliefs must be identified and changed.

Only YOU are responsible for your thoughts and beliefs. Only YOU can control what thoughts dominate your thinking. Only YOU can make the necessary changes. BELIEVE you have the power within yourself, no matter your age or circumstances, to turn your dreams into your reality.

For Further Thought:

What's Really Holding You Back?

1. Think about the common self-limiting beliefs I've described
    in this chapter. Which ones apply to you?

    _____

    _____

    _____

    _____

    _____

    _____

    _____

    _____

    _____

2. When you examined a recent decision, what self-limiting
    beliefs do you think you used in the process of making the
    decision?

    _____

    _____

    _____

    _____

    _____

    _____

    _____

    _____

    _____

    _____

    _____

3. How are these belief systems keeping you from achieving your goals? For example, are you too likely to avoid risk because of the negative messages you heard when you were a child?

    _____
    _____
    _____
    _____
    _____
    _____
    _____
    _____
    _____
    _____

4. Consider how you can begin to eliminate your self-limiting beliefs. What specific actions can you take? For example, can you refuse to emotionally react, and internalize every negative message you hear on the television or radio or from friends?

    _____
    _____
    _____
    _____
    _____
    _____
    _____
    _____
    _____
    _____
    _____

5.   Positive affirmation statements which reinforce your decision to change your beliefs can be very helpful. Develop positive statements for your key self-limiting beliefs. Following are some examples to adapt as needed.

- I AM capable of changing my thinking in order to change my results

- I AM worthy of living my perfect life

- Life's a game and I AM great at playing the game

Create your own affirmations below:

_____
_____
_____
_____
_____
_____
_____
_____
_____
_____
_____
_____
_____

*If you don't want to write in your book... You can download all the exercises at:
www.TheMoneyMirrorBook.com/resources

Rae Brent

Chapter 4

The Shocking Truth About Overnight Success!

Once we commit to change, we tend to expect immediate results. While it's a good idea to start thinking positively about taking control of your finances. It can be disappointing when it takes a little longer than you expected.

If you were honest with yourself, you would know that you didn't arrive at your financial situation overnight, so it's probably unrealistic to think it will change overnight.

Even if you're sticking to your plan, you may find it taking longer than you hoped to chip away at your debt.

The fact that interest keeps piling up, while you work to pay down balances on credit cards, for example, can be disheartening. Maybe you've been less committed to your plan than you hoped, catching yourself overspending and falling into other problem habits.

If you are frustrated by the pace of change or if you can't seem to stay in control, I want to encourage you to keep at it. Everyone has found themselves taking detours from their chosen path now and then. The key is to get back on track as quickly as possible. If you feel you're moving too slowly, consider tweaking your plan, but NEVER GIVE UP!

By falling back into old and damaging financial patterns, you may be digging yourself into an even deeper hole. The larger your debts become, the more difficult it is to pay them off. This results in more of your money being used to pay off your debts before you can begin to save and invest.

Let's begin by identifying some of the most common pitfalls and how you can get back on track. Some of these problems can originate with us—in the messages we are internalizing or in our lack of commitment to breaking old patterns; in fact, we can be our own worst enemy.

At other times, the issue involves others around us. Finally, the problem may be a legitimate issue through an investment by a financial professional on your behalf. It's worthwhile considering that *"nobody else looks after your money as good as you can."*

This is the main reason why it is important to educate yourself in the investment vehicles that you choose to drive. When all is said and done, you are the one responsible for what your money is doing.

What Messages Are You Sending Yourself?

One thing we do to ourselves is revert to old self-limiting beliefs. These may be so ingrained, we don't even realize they're affecting us.

Go back over your limiting beliefs and reconsider how they may still be at work. They may be causing you to spend more than is good for your financial plan. Or they may be keeping you from feeling confident enough to make other strides along the path toward your ideal life.

They may be at work at a level so deep that you don't even recognize them. Sometimes we are inadvertently reinforcing them with the messages we expose ourselves to and the emotional responses we make. You may also be reinforcing a negative mindset or setting the stage for moving in the wrong direction with the information and messages you're sending yourself.

In the 1930s, Dr Thurman Fleet developed an illustration later used and made popular by Bob Proctor. This stick person example describes the relationship between our conscious and subconscious minds. It is important to understand this relationship so that you can avoid sabotaging your own best efforts at success.

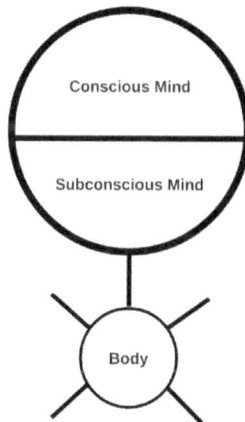

The top circle, or head, represents the mind or thoughts; the bottom circle represents the body or actions. The top circle is divided into two halves to represent the conscious mind and the subconscious mind.

Some of my mentors refer to this top circle as our *Necktop Computer*. I really love this terminology. When we put it into perspective of our everyday lives, just as we can add, delete and edit programs on our desktop or laptop computers, we can also do the same in our necktop computer – our mind.

I've taken this concept one step further to the stage that with any computer, at some point in time when it is not working to its full potential, we invariably run a *defragmentation* program to streamline its operations and create more available space for empowering programs (belief systems) to be added.

When was the last time you *defragged* your necktop computer?

The conscious mind receives input from the world around us. When we encounter new information, our conscious minds have the ability to accept or reject the new ideas. The conscious mind constantly filters the images coming to us from our environment.

Our conscious mind allows us to choose which ideas and events we want to become emotionally involved in, and we have the power to shape our responses. The conscious mind is also the location where we make plans and set goals.

Every day, we are exposed to thousands of images from the media and our daily lives. Information streams at us from the television, radio, internet, print media, the people around us, and elsewhere.

We can only consciously process a fraction of this information. Although you may not realize it, you are constantly choosing which images you will process and accept into your own reality.

Whilst our conscious minds are amazing filters, it is important to protect them. Our conscious minds are constantly bombarded with negative messages, both from the outside world (just think about the daily news for one) and from our own self talk (self judgment). Some of these messages will eventually filter through to our subconscious mind. Once this happens, we tend to become negative people with pessimistic attitudes and negative opinions.

To change this process, we must guard against inundating ourselves with negative messages. Be careful of the images you expose yourself to; this also extends to include the people you hang around. Choose to become emotionally engaged in more positive directions and with more positive people. There is an old saying that *"Your Network is your Networth,"* so start hanging around people that you want to be like.

In this way, you can help your conscious mind and, in turn, better enable it to do its job of protecting your subconscious mind.

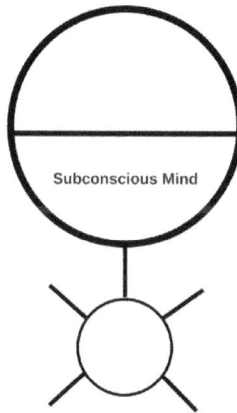

The subconscious mind is the *emotional mind* or *feeling mind*. Unlike the conscious mind, the subconscious mind has no ability to filter information.

The subconscious mind does not understand such terms as: not, try, don't or can't. So, when we tell ourselves (using self talk) that *"I don't want to lose my job, house, partner... etc."* our subconscious mind only hears the command … *"I want to lose my job, house, partner …. etc."*

My business partner, Pauline Longdon, is a great example of this A few years ago, when she was a Nursing Officer in the Australian Army, she witnessed many military personnel being discharged for psychological reasons.

Pauline started to say to herself and to others around her that she didn't want to be discharged from the Military on a *"Psych Discharge."*

You guessed it. A few short years later, after back to back overseas deployments, she was diagnosed with Major Depression.

Pauline's *wish* certainly came true and she was psychologically discharged from the Military suffering from Major Depression. Pauline now focuses on what she does want in life.

The subconscious minds' job is to answer any command it receives from the conscious mind. James Arthur Ray tells us that it replies like a genie with, *"Your wish is my command!"* as seen in the DVD movie *The Secret.*

Each one of us is great at manifesting things into our lives. Unfortunately, most of us manifest the things that we don't want easier than what we do want.

There are two simple reasons for this:

1. We are driven by fear and focus solely on what we don't want in our lives (this is how society has programmed us to perform); and

2. We are unable to be definitive about what we do want in life. A lot of issues that I find responsible for this are that on some level we do not believe we deserve to be happy or to have the perfect lifestyle we desire.

A Quick Exercise: Write down on a piece of paper, in 100 words or more, what your perfect life would look like if you could have it all right now.

Were you able to write down 100 words or more? Can you define what you do want as opposed to what you don't want in your life? Keep playing with the idea, that the more definitive you become with what you do want, the easier it'll be for the universe to provide it for you.

Now because the subconscious mind is unable to accept or reject thoughts. You must make every effort to limit the negative thoughts and feelings you allow into your conscious mind.

So, if fear, worry, anger, or any other negative emotions enter your subconscious mind, they can cause you to move in the wrong direction.

You see, if you worry about something happening, you take it into your subconscious mind. And the subconscious mind can then move you in the direction of the very thing you fear!

For example. Imagine you are afraid you're going to lose your job. Imagine this fear makes you so nervous and defensive that you start to change your behavior. You become increasingly difficult to work with as you filter every comment or action by your co-workers through your fear.

You agonize over the latest rumors on the office grapevine. You may find your temper grows shorter. And your work quality declines *(why work hard when you're about to be fired?)* Your negative attitude becomes apparent to your customers and co-workers.

Over time, your behavior shapes the feelings of the people around you. It's not hard to imagine things getting so bad that you DO get fired.

By internalizing your negative assumptions and your worry, you affect your subconscious mind. It can respond in powerful ways, but it tends to move in the direction it is encouraged to go by your conscious mind. If the direction is fear and worry, you may find yourself moving in the direction of those fears.

On the other hand, we can influence our subconscious mind to move us in the direction of the things we do want in life by focusing on surrounding ourselves with images and thoughts of those things. If our conscious mind is filled with positive things, our subconscious mind will be too, and we will move in positive directions.

Consider, for example, a worker who consistently demonstrates a *"can-do"* attitude. Easy to get along with and always willing to help, this person is a favorite among their co-workers and customers. Such an individual is more secure in their job thanks to the positive energy they are putting forth.

The Law of Attraction, an idea made popular by Bob Proctor and incorporated in the movie *"The Secret"* by Rhonda Byrne. Tells us that if we put out positive energy, we will attract good things into our lives.

The same is true for negative energy; it will attract more negative energy. By focusing on what you don't want, you can bring more of what you don't want into your life.

How many times have you manifested negative things into your reality? It's time to change your thinking and attract the things that you do want to materialize into your life.

If you find that you aren't changing your financial situation as quickly as you would like, be sure you are putting the right messages in place. Surround yourself with positive images and people and work to choose to emotionally respond to the information and situations that move you toward your goals.

You can also purposefully direct your powerful subconscious mind to aid in creating your perfect life. Add, edit or remove the programs you want in your necktop computer and allow yourself to take control of your financial situation.

Manifest your dreams and remove the blocks that are stopping you from having them in your life right now. Positive or negative thoughts and attitudes can become self-fulfilling, just as Pauline found out.

Whichever way you choose to do it… Decide – Commit – Act (and just you do it!)

As Henry Ford said…

If you think you can or think you can't
…You are 100% right!

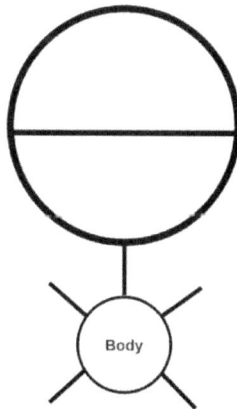

The body, represented by the lower circle, carries out actions based on directions from the conscious and subconscious minds. It is the physical manifestation of our dominant thoughts and is created and recreated daily. It is also the visible evidence of what is held in the mind.

An often-used example of this involves public speaking. Imagine you're about to give a speech. If you worry about being nervous, saying something inappropriate, or are concerned that someone will make fun of you, then your body will manifest those thoughts. Your palms will begin to sweat; you'll stumble over your words and you'll feel very embarrassed.

However, if you spend time imagining how positively your audience will respond, how articulate you will sound and how energized you will feel, the body will manifest that as well. You will be confident and full of energy, and your audience can't help but respond positively to you.

When we intentionally change the thoughts to which we give the most focus and energy to in our conscious mind, they are then impressed upon our subconscious mind. They then become emotions, our body puts those emotions into action, and our actions become our results.

If you've been unhappy with your financial situation for an extended period, you are probably in the habit of focusing on the negative aspects of it. For example, you may be constantly worried and fearful.

In addition to making you miserable, these negative thoughts and emotions are being fed into your subconscious mind. Since it cannot say *"no,"* it reacts to this negativity by attracting even more bad things your way.

To look at another example of the links between the conscious mind, the subconscious mind and the body, think of a relationship you have with another person that is very close to you. This could be a parent, child, spouse, or other loved one. If you allow yourself to respond to negative images, what happens?

Imagine your child doesn't clean up their room (again!) or walk the dog (again!) and you become emotionally responsive to those facts, feeding your subconscious mind these negative signals. You may also feel your stress level rising and your temper getting shorter.

You may develop a headache as your anger rises. The child senses your feelings and becomes grouchy and withdrawn. This makes you even angrier! Before you know it, you have a raging headache and have yelled at the child and then every time you ask the child to do a task, you get angry.

These cycles can become self-fulfilling. Growing ever more damaging to you and those around you. By contrast, you could choose to shut the door on the negative feelings in the early stages. If you filter out the negative emotions and consciously decide to RESPOND to the situation instead of REACT-ing in an emotional way, you can minimize the fallout.

In the context of your financial situation, your conscious mind is bombarded with images. Choose them with care.

As noted previously, bad news abounds in the media and elsewhere. If you surround yourself with these negative statements and then react to them, they are being fed into your subconscious mind. If you feel pessimistic about the economy and your job prospects, for instance, you may pass up good opportunities.

Sir Richard Branson says it best when he says…

Opportunities are like buses...
There will be another one coming
around the corner in 10 minutes

If you're unhappy with your progress so far, begin to change the messages you are letting into your subconscious mind. Focus on positive news and encouraging ideas. Protect your subconscious mind. Don't let it turn into a force moving you in the wrong direction.

Instead, keep it in alignment with your dreams and goals by focusing on them and the fact that you are taking control of your finances to move closer to your ideal financial life. And remember that you deserve to achieve your dreams, goals and aspirations in every area of your life. It's your Birthright!

Have You Taken The Time And Effort To Change Your Habits?

There are different theories about the length of time it takes to change a habit. Some experts believe you can make a real change in around three weeks. I've also heard estimates of a little longer than that. I've even heard a school teacher say that it can take up to 100 repetitions for some kids to pick up a new idea. So even if you take the fastest estimate (21 days), it's still a substantial length of time.

Moreover, it takes real effort on your part as well as the decision to change. Old habits, as they say, die hard. We have ingrained our patterns over long spans of time. They may be tied to our pasts, our current relationships, and our beliefs about ourselves. Sometimes just coming up with a goal isn't enough. You may have to take the time to do some retraining to break habits such as overspending.

Bad habits may also be feeding negative images into your subconscious mind through the linkages previously described. If you see a habit you're having trouble breaking, take control of the behavior and make a plan to change it.

Decide to change it. Commit to taking the appropriate action to change it. And then take the appropriate action required. *Decide – Commit – Act.*

Here's one plan for changing habits which I've used in the past. It's a simple one. Because sometimes all it takes is a little awareness of the habit. And then a bit of effort and some time to change it.

The first step in breaking a habit is to define it precisely. This may be more difficult than you think. The more specific you can get, the easier it is to effectively stop the habit. For example, if you tend to overspend, it will be hard to break a habit you think of as *"overspending."* That's far too broad a term to deal with.

Instead, take a more detailed look at the kinds of things you tend to overspend on and why. If, for example, your weakness is expensive clothes, and you tend to buy them because you are in the habit of walking through the exclusive shopping area near your office on your lunch hour, your goal may be to stop walking through the shops and start walking through the park instead.

Look for the underlying causes of the habit. In this case, the underlying causes are likely to be the habit of walking through the shops and trying to make yourself happy.

A way to make these changes easier is to prioritize the problem habits and tackle them one by one. Rather than trying to change everything at the same time, start with the one thing that's doing the most harm. When you have it under control, you can move to the next one on your list.

Success is more likely when the changes are incremental. It may take a little more time, but the probability that you'll stick with the plan is higher than if you totally rearrange your life overnight.

So, once you have defined the habit you want to change, write it down. The next step is to define what you want to do instead of that habit. *"I want to walk through the park and get some healthy exercise during my lunch break."*

Next, remember all the reasons you want to break the habit. Think about how it is keeping you from moving toward your goals. Think how it affects your image in *The Money Mirror*.

Writing down the most important reasons can also be helpful. If there is something that stands out in your mind when you picture your perfect life (a peaceful cabin in the woods, a shiny new car, or some other possession), write that down as well.

Affirmations can be very helpful in the process of breaking habits. There are countless books, articles and even DVDs filled with positive affirmations that you can use right away. I find lists of affirmations a great resource, because I don't have to spend hours coming up with them on my own.

If you feel the temptation to fall back into your old habit, look for other beliefs attached to the habit. Also, find others who can and will support your personal development.

If you do find yourself repeating a habit, it may be a belief that's held in a deeper level of your conscious mind. If you find you're not getting you the results you expect, you may need someone to help you.

Are Your Beliefs Supporting Your Dreams?

One reason for not having achieved your dreams now is, your current belief system isn't in alignment with you. And the best thing about belief systems is they're just B.S. And they can easily be changed to support your desires.

There's no need to get attached to old beliefs that are holding you back from achieving greatness. Identify them quickly and then change them.

While it's a great idea to set high standards and dream big, remember to set stepping stones in place along the way.

This way, you'll be setting yourself up for success instead of failure. And start to celebrate your small achievements along the way. The more you're grateful for in life, the more things will be presented to you to be grateful for. Because, *"what you appreciate, appreciates!"*

Look at your progress compared to your chosen path. What beliefs are stopping you from having your perfect life now? Ask yourself the question *"If I had ... (Insert your dream here) in my life now, what is the worst thing about having that?"* (Do you have to give it all away to your family? Do you fear losing it all?)

Now just pause for a moment and allow your subconscious mind to come up with all the limiting beliefs you have that are stopping you from having everything you want in your life now.

Are You Getting The Support You Need?

In some cases, the underlying problem with moving forward is that some members of the household are not as committed as they must be to make it all work. If your spouse won't stay within the allocated budget, for example, it can throw off your entire plan.

The sort of relationship advice you may need to work through such issues could be well beyond the scope of this book. However, sometimes the problem is as simple as stepping back for a moment and taking the time to discuss your ultimate financial goals and recalibrating your relationship towards that goal. After all, if you're part of a family, some component of your goals likely involves providing for the family, increasing the time you can spend with them, or being able to afford to treat them to the things wealth can provide.

If differences of opinion cannot be worked through with negotiation, it can be very painful. Without the support of all family members, it can be almost impossible to take control of your finances.

Each of us has a responsibility for our own wellbeing—physically, emotionally, spiritually, and financially. It can be very hard to come to an agreement about how money is spent. If you find yourself working hard to pay down debt only to have your spouse go out and run up more, it can be very frustrating and painful.

Money problems are at the heart of many relationship issues, but the reverse can also be true. Relationship difficulties can be the one cause of financial problems. So, unless all persons involved are committed to the same goals, achieving them may be difficult (if not impossible.)

For Further Thought:

The Shocking Truth About Overnight Success!

1. Think back to the roots of your financial problems. How long ago would you say they started? Remember that it's taken you since that time to reach the point where you are now.

    _____
    _____
    _____
    _____
    _____

2. Think about the images you were bombarded with today from the media and your daily life. Which ones did you react emotionally to and why?

    _____
    _____
    _____
    _____
    _____
    _____

3. Do you think the images and ideas were positive or negative? Why?

    _____
    _____
    _____
    _____
    _____

4. How can you better control the negative images you are faced with?

5. How can you increase the positive images and ideas you surround yourself with?

6. What difference do you think that could make?

7.   What habits and beliefs are keeping you from attaining your goals?

_____

_____

_____

_____

_____

_____

_____

8.   For each problem habit and belief you have, what do you want instead?

_____

_____

_____

_____

_____

_____

_____

_____

_____

_____

_____

Commit to changing your old beliefs. Because they are no longer serving you.

*If you don't want to write in your book... You can download all the exercises at:
www.TheMoneyMirrorBook.com/resources

Rae Brent

Chapter 5

How To Take Your Financial Snapshot

An assessment of your current financial status is important for you take control of your money situation. A snapshot-style look at your income, expenses, assets, and debts can provide essential guidance in the process of formulating a plan to get control of your finances and begin to build real wealth.

Once you have a current snapshot, you can begin to project where you will be in the future if you stay on your current path. While the future will, of course, be impossible to know with certainty, you can nonetheless determine whether you're likely to be moving closer to your goals and dreams or farther away.

The major phases of taking the snapshot are...

- Gathering the necessary information

- Compiling your financial data

- Drawing conclusions about your current situation

- Looking to the future

- Assessing whether your current financial mindset is getting you where you want to go in life

The goals of this process are not only to increase your understanding of your finances, but also to enhance your comfort level with where you are and where you're going. In this way, you can identify the ways money is keeping you from living the life you want to live.

Information Gathering

The first major step in taking your financial snapshot is to gather information. This can seem somewhat overwhelming, so I've broken it down into two major categories: What you OWN and what you OWE. The next step is to look at what comes IN as income from various sources and what goes OUT in the form of expenses.

A Note About Timing

As you collect your account balances, and the other data you need for your financial snapshot. You'll want to think about the timing of your analysis. You'll need to choose a specific date and work to get all your balances as of that day.

This should be in the past enough for you to already have bank statements, credit card bills, account values, and other relevant pieces of data on hand. Sometimes it's easiest to pick the first day of a month and get all your figures current as of that date.

Sometimes, it's difficult to get balances as of a specific date. Various investment accounts, for example, may not value shares daily. Most of the time, it won't make a big difference if the *"as-of"* dates vary to a small degree. Many balances are relatively stable, and a few days one way or the other won't cause any huge problems.

Choose a date to take your snapshot, then work through the list and start rounding up your underlying paperwork. Then you'll enter the amounts into a worksheet and take a look. You'll need to make some adjustments for your situation; you may have different assets or debts. The key is to think through all the various things you own and owe and bring them together for your snapshot.

It's also helpful to gather balances for the past six months or so to look at patterns for the future. In some cases, putting together data going even farther back will be desirable.

If you begin to feel overwhelmed by stacks of paper, however, just cut it back to the most recent. As you become more comfortable with looking at your finances, it will be easier to be more specific and look at a longer period. If all you want to tackle at first is last month, start there. You can build on that next time you look in *The Money Mirror.*

For most people, a few accounts or assets / debts are the keys to their snapshot, providing a decent view of the situation even though they don't represent every single item. You can get started by looking at just a handful of the larger ticket items and probably come close to your true money reflection. It's great to be precise and thorough, but don't let getting caught up in each detail keep you from getting going.

Once you begin to get comfortable with looking at your finances, you will be able to drill down to the smaller ticket items (which may be a big part of your current financial issues.)

Remember to keep emotions away from what you see. Live without harshly judging your current situation or regretting past decisions that have led you to where you are.

Realistically, is anyone going to die if your financial snap shot is a couple of dollars out! What you are doing is getting an overall picture of your money situation, not micro-managing it down to the last cent.

A Note About Current Values

As you put together the values of the things you own, it is important to think in terms of their value if you decided to sell them. For purposes of your financial snapshot, what you originally paid is not relevant, neither is what it would cost to replace them.

It is also not a measure of what the things you own are worth to you, as they may have sentimental or emotional value far beyond the price you could get for them. What is relevant is what you could sell the items for to someone else.

When you begin to look at the current values of items you own, such as your personal property. It's not all that helpful to try to put a dollar figure on each t-shirt in your drawer or plate in your kitchen.

Stick to the big things at first. If you have a collection of valuable coins, for example, you might want to include that in your financial snapshot. And while any and everything you own may have value to someone else, it's helpful to start with the big things. You can always add more details later.

You may also have some concern about coming up with values, even if you simplify down to the most important items. But remember, there are resources available to can help you.

For real estate assets including houses, buildings, raw land, or anything else, you can look at the selling prices for comparable assets. If you're looking at the value of a house, for example, check the newspaper listings to see if there are any similar homes with prices. Your local newspaper probably has articles about what houses are selling for.

There are also organizations that track sales and prices which you may be able to contact for prices. Sometimes, real estate salespeople offer free valuations as part of their services in hopes you would use them as agents if you decided to sell (or buy.) For cars, boats, motorcycles, or other major items, you can also check newspaper listings or internet sites.

If You Own A Business

The value of a business can be more difficult to estimate. While a full discussion of business valuation is clearly beyond the scope of this book, there are several very good resources available with step-by-step methods for determining the value of businesses. There are also hundreds of firms and individuals providing valuation services.

If a business is a major component of your financial picture and you don't have a clear idea of its value, it can make it impossible to understand your money situation, and I would highly recommend further study of this issue.

It's also crucial to analyze the business and its profit potential, ability to generate income for you, and possible future sales price. I see people spend many, many hours on businesses that are not profitable or valuable. It's also possible to get so involved in your company that you no longer see its role in your happiness or finances clearly.

I once watched a friend put everything she had - heart, soul, and bank account - into her small business. She nurtured it and worked it and watched it lose money. Unwilling to be realistic, she kept hoping that it would turn the corner and make a profit, but it never did.

The bottom line is that owning a business complicates your financial snapshot in several ways. If you already have strong business and strategic plans in place, you may have identified the financial potential of you company. If not, you should consider going through that process and / or seek professional advice as needed.

Putting Together "What I Own"

Use the following checklist to help with collecting information about your assets. Note that some of these categories won't change very rapidly or frequently.

For example: If the real estate market in your area is stable, the value of your house may not change rapidly. However, other types of assets (such as shares) can fluctuate on a daily basis.

My point is. You need to get enough information about the values over time to know whether they are stable or changing. And, if they are changing. You need to know in what direction they're changing.

What I Own Necessary Information	
	✔
Statements and/or Balances for the Past 6 Months	
Bank Account(s)	
Savings Account(s)	
Retirement Account(s)	
Investment Account(s)	
Other shares, securities, bonds, or financial investments	
Current Values *(These figures should be what you could SELL these items for, not what it would cost to REPLACE them.)*	
House and other real estate	
Car(s)	
Boats, motorcycles, etc.	
Personal Property (jewelry, furnishings, art)	
Cash values of insurance policies	
Business Interests	
Other Assets	

Again, you will almost certainly have other types of assets. Use this checklist to get started, aim for capturing data on the largest and most valuable things you own, and add to your set of information as needed.

Putting Together "What I Owe"

The other side of your personal balance sheet is what you owe. Below is a checklist to help you collect the necessary paperwork.

Many times, assembling data on what you owe is simplified by the fact there are others (namely those people or companies you owe the money) who are keeping up with the precise amounts and timelines.

What I Owe Necessary Information	
	✔
Statements and/or Balances for the Past 6 Months	
House loan(s)	
Car loan(s)	
Business loan(s)	
Credit Card balance(s)	
Student loans(s)	
Medical bills	
Obligations for taxes	
Other personal loans	

What you owe should cover all outstanding debts of various types.

Analyzing "What's Coming In"

The next step in looking in *The Money Mirror* is to look at money coming in each month. These inflows are what allow you to build assets and sustainable wealth. For some people, inflows are relatively simple: they get a payment from an employer on a particular day (or days) of each month.

For others, however, their inflows can vary widely. Many salespeople are paid based on their sales volumes, for example. Business owners may be paid based on the profitability of the business that month. People working by the hour may see sizable variation in the number of hours worked and, hence, their cash inflows for the month. Those with investment portfolios may also see widely different inflows depending on factors such as the types of investments they hold, market performance, and so on.

Some of the required information for analyzing your inflows will be contained in the statements and documents related to your assets. In addition, you'll need to assemble other things, such as those on the following checklist.

What Comes In Necessary Information	
	✔
Monthly Inflows for the Past 6 Months	
Wage/Salary: Primary job	
Wage/Salary: Other job(s)	
Investment income	
Rental income	

Retirement income	
Other regular payments	

These inflows should represent regular payments that you expect to continue to receive in the future. They should be regular, recurring inflows that you have no reason to believe will end in the short term. Some payments are of a one-time nature, such as when you sell something. It's important not to confuse these unusual events with your regular inflows.

Analyzing "What's Going Out"

The next phase of putting together your financial snapshot is to review the money going out each month. Many people are very surprised by this portion of the financial snapshot. Certain payments are typically well defined (such as the house loan or rental payment that's due every month) and well known.

If you add up the payments you can think of off the top of your head that you must make each month, however, they usually don't account for anything approaching your total expenses. Where does the extra go? Sometimes, we underestimate what we spend for necessities such as food. You know you go to the grocery store or restaurant, but do you keep a running total in mind for the month?

Even more enlightening can be the level of payments for other things. The small bits of cash you shell out over the month for coffees or parking charges or movie tickets can add up. The interest charges on your credit cards can also be another sizable outflow.

Since most of us don't do a great job with keeping up with these expenses in our heads, it's necessary to devote some time to compiling this data (if you don't already.) There are several good software programs available that let you categorize each expenditure, so you can see how much you're spending for various types of things. Some credit card companies do a decent job helping you with this, too.

If you don't already track your expenses and know where your money goes, it's well worth the effort - at least on occasion. This is where you can really begin to see one of the biggest reasons money is making you unhappy. You can see where you're spending for things that aren't important to you. You may be surprised by what you find.

I hope that you're already committed to taking the time to put your outflow information together. If you've already worked through the other pieces of your financial snapshot, you should certainly keep the momentum going.

However, it can be tempting to skip over taking a hard look at your expenses, and I want to encourage you NOT to omit this important view in *The Money Mirror*.

My friend Kate had always made ends meet. She wasn't living the life she really wanted, but she was at least keeping her head above water in terms of her finances.

As she watched me work on my real estate investment program and other wealth-building strategies, we began to have discussions about money and how to have more of it. Her dream was to be able to stop working the long hours she was putting in and be able to spend more time with her kids, but she felt she needed to have more money in the bank first.

When I asked Kate to think about the money that came in every month, she could easily come up with a total. (I found out later that even after she sat down and took a thorough look, she was close.)

The next question I asked her to think about was how much she was saving each month; in other words, what was being added to her wealth each month. The answer was basically zero. While she would get some money put aside for a few months, something would come up and it would be spent. The car would need a service, or she'd take a small vacation and she'd be back to zero.

We then talked about Kate's expenses. When she attempted to tally up the amount going out in her head, she couldn't get anywhere close to her monthly income. She knew her rent and her car repayment and some other big items that were the same each month.

Kate guessed at the amounts she had a good idea of, such as the usual monthly bills for utilities. She guessed at her spending for groceries and clothes and everything else she could think of, but she wasn't close.

It was only after she sat down and got very specific that she was able to figure out where her money was going. And after carefully tracking spending for several months, Kate began to see she had several habits costing her more than she realized.

The coffee bar downstairs in the building where she worked was one culprit. While she enjoyed her latte, she decided she'd rather have a plain coffee and save that money. Several of the totals surprised her and helped her get back on track toward reaching her financial goals.

Make a commitment to take the time to really look at your expenses. One of the most important ways you can begin to build wealth is by really understanding your expenses and doing all you can to be sure they reflect your underlying money goals. If you're wasting money on things that aren't making you happy, you're only cheating yourself.

Put together this information, even though it may take you some time. I've seen it make such a difference in people's lives.

What Goes Out Necessary Information	
	✔
Statements and/or Balances for the Past 6 Months	
Housing payments (loan payments or rent)	
Car loan/lease payments	
Business loan payments	
Student loan payments	
Tuition payments	
Other loan payments	
Utility payments (electricity/power, telecommunications, water, other)	
Groceries/eating out	
Clothing and personal items	
Entertainment	
Insurance payments	
Other spending	

You will certainly have many other categories of expenses. They will be driven by your own situation and preferences. Decide on the categories that are meaningful to you and notate them as appropriate.

Hopefully, there's an amount you're setting aside in the form of wealth creation. For example, you may be making monthly transfers from your regular bank account into your savings or investments.

If it becomes confusing, you can set up a category on your sheet of *"What Goes Out"* to represent these transfers (which are additions to your wealth creation) and account for the differences between what's coming in on a regular basis (your income) and what's going out (your expenses.)

The goal is for you to have the information you need to take your financial snapshot. Do you feel you have everything together? If not, pull together the missing pieces and let's get it started.

Compiling The Data

Before you can take your financial snapshot, you'll need to organize what you've gathered together. There are numerous ways to do this; some are simple, and some are complicated. There are many very powerful software packages you can buy for your computer that let you put all this information in and get a bottom line number. There are financial planning firms that will help you for a fee. You can get as detailed and complex as you wish.

It is important, though, to keep it simple enough so that you can really get your brain around it and draw some conclusions. You already have what may be hundreds of pages describing your finances. The difficulty is that it's hard to see the *"big picture."* There are so many individual pieces that it's hard to identify the meaningful patterns.

While a very detailed look may suit your personality well and be exactly right for you, there are benefits to simplicity. If you can get a grasp of the situation with an overview, you can always dig deeper into the problem areas you find.

My experience has shown me that people usually don't have to look very long in *The Money Mirror* to begin to spot the problems. Better to go ahead and get going and then go back for more detail than to peck away trying to capture every detail and never get to the point where you attempt to see the big picture.

Here's one way to get a financial snapshot. Again, start with the basics and go back and fill in as needed. You'll need paper, pencil, and a calculator or a spreadsheet software package on your computer. For each major category, sort out the information you collected and make a list of the relevant amounts. If the details start to seem overwhelming to you, back off and get down the largest and most important things first.

Here's an example of what your *"What I Own"* sheet might look like.

What I Own						
Asset Value if Sold	**Jan 1**	**Feb 1**	**Mar 1**	**Apr 1**	**May 1**	**Jun 1**
House	$400,000	$400,000	$400,000	$400,000	$400,000	$400,000
Cars	$20,000	$20,000	$20,000	$20,000	$20,000	$20,000
Furniture and household	$8,000	$8,000	$8,000	$8,000	$8,000	$8,000
Other	$12,000	$10,000	$11,000	$12,000	$11,000	$12,000
Investment account	$22,000	$25,000	$24,500	$24,000	$25,000	$27,000
Retirement account	$14,000	$14,500	$15,000	$15,500	$16,000	$16,500
TOTAL	$476,000	$477,500	$478,500	$479,500	$480,000	$483,500

Once you have the major line items and have totaled them up, move on to the same exercise for *"What I Owe."*

After you've organized your information for your assets (What I Own) and debts (What I Owe), compile your monthly income and expense information into similar worksheets. Start with the largest categories and move into the detail from there.

Taking The Snapshot

As you assemble these financial documents, you will begin to see a picture emerge. You see what you own lined up next to what you owe. There is money coming in and money going out. So how do you put it all together?

Divide a single sheet of paper into quarters. Label the upper left quarter *"What I Own"* and the upper right quarter *"What I Owe."*

Then label the lower left quarter *"What Comes In"* and the lower right quarter *"What Goes Out."* See the following diagram.

What I Own	What I Owe
What Comes In	**What Goes Out**

In each quadrant, you'll summarize key findings in each area.

Look back over your lists of organized assets, debt, income, and expenses. Are the patterns stable over the months you're analyzing? If so, you can just choose the most recent value or entry.

If the patterns are not stable, look to the reasons they're changing. Was there a notable change in a category? You may need to go with the most recent (if there was an unusual event such as purchasing a new house) or you may need to calculate an average (if it's varying due to changing market conditions, for instance.)

If there is a discernible trend, you should certainly go with the most recent entry unless you have reason to believe the trend will change. For example, if the value of your investment account is rising steadily due (in part) to your monthly contributions to it, you would go with the latest value rather than an average.

Ensure you're dealing with the issues we discussed previously—the things that can keep you from seeing clearly. As you come up with the value of your house, try not to be too optimistic (if that's your personality) or overly pessimistic (if that's more your style.) Go with your best estimate, adjusting for the types of things that keep you from getting a reliable image.

Remember, most Real Estate Agents will conduct a FREE Appraisal if you ask.

Also, realize that 100% perfection isn't possible. None of us can know what the markets are going to do or what your employer may decide about next year's raises or whether your expenses could jump for some unexpected reason.

Even if you achieved the standard of 100% perfection today, it would be out of date immediately and you'd need to reassess all the time.

Keep in mind your goal here: to get a picture of your money situation. It won't be 100% complete or 100% accurate, but it can still help you begin to take charge of your personal finances.

Drawing Conclusions

As you look at your divided paper with its summary of:

- What you own,

- What you owe,

- What comes in, and

- What goes out.

What patterns can you see? Ask yourself questions like these…

- Are you happy and encouraged by what you see? Do you feel comfortable with where you stand? Is it better or worse than you expected?

- Is the total amount you own larger than the total amount you owe?

  - If you answered *"yes,"* good for you! That's an important first step in taking control of your financial situation.

  - If not, why not? Is there some large debt that you're paying off that doesn't have a corresponding asset? For example, the loan for your house (if you have one) is offset by the value of your house. Hopefully, the value of your house is even larger than the loan for your house. However, there are some debts that don't have an offsetting asset you can sell. For example, if you have student loans or medical bills you are paying off, there won't be an offsetting asset.

- Is the total coming in larger than the total going out?

    ○ If *"yes,"* that's good news. If you're bringing in more in the form of income than you're sending out by way of your expenses, you are in a good starting point.

    ○ If *"no,"* how so? Is there some temporary reason your income is low? Have your expenses been unusually high? How big is the difference?

What are you seeing as you look into *The Money Mirror?* Are you in better shape than you feared? Is it worse than you thought?

Would you like to improve what you see? Believe me, you can. Don't be discouraged by bad news (if that's what you got), though maybe it provided you with a necessary reality check. It's difficult (if not impossible) to build real, sustainable wealth if you are out of touch with your situation. It is better to face it, see it clearly, and then work on changing it to be what you want it to be.

About The Future

Before we leave your snapshot, take some time to think about the likely future direction of your finances. As noted, you can't possibly foretell the future. However, as you look over your data, you can see trends in some variables. Based on these trends, you can make some educated guesses about the general direction you're moving. Is it getting better or worse?

Staying clear of the details for the moment, can you get a feel for the general pattern? Would you give it a *"thumbs up"* or a *"thumbs down?"* As you look at your financial snapshot, your conclusions may partly be driven by future expectations.

Later in the book, I'll help you figure out whether your financial direction is a good fit for your own definition of success and path to happiness. For now, just let yourself think in general terms about the direction you're going.

Do You Like What You See?

Check your emotional state right now. Are you feeling better than you were when you started this process? If so, great! Let's figure out how to make it even better.

If not, take heart. By working through this financial snapshot, you've provided yourself with valuable tools you can use to begin to get control of your money situation and build real wealth. You will have a better idea of the good things and bad things going on in your *Money Mirror.* You may be more organized with your financial records. Perhaps you've already begun to find some problem areas.

In knowing where you stand, there is power. You can't take charge of what you don't understand. If you were overwhelmed or confused by money, you have probably already begun to deal with those issues.

Note: For a simple and quick way to get your finances under control. I have an online course called "Discipline Your Dollars to Get Out of Debt" (at www.DisciplineYourDollars.com). The course is filled with useful tools, tips and resources you can use to change your reflection in *The Money Mirror.*

For Further Thought:

How To Take Your Financial Snapshot

1. What was your biggest surprise as you put together your financial information?

    _____

    _____

    _____

    _____

    _____

    _____

2. How close were you to what you expected to find when you looked in your *Money Mirror?*

    _____

    _____

    _____

    _____

    _____

    _____

    _____

3. Are you happy with what you saw?

    _____

    _____

    _____

    _____

    _____

4. Are you better off or worse off than you expected?

_____
_____
_____
_____

5. If you think about what you would like to change, what is the first thing that pops into your head? Why?

_____
_____
_____
_____
_____
_____

6. What connections can you begin to draw between what you saw in your *Money Mirror* and how your CURRENT life is not your PERFECT life?

_____
_____
_____
_____
_____
_____
_____

*If you don't want to write in your book… You can download all the exercises at:
www.TheMoneyMirrorBook.com/resources

Chapter 6

Are You Happy With What You See?

N ow that you've taken a look in *The Money Mirror*, are you happy with your reflection? Or did you find yourself asking, *"Is this what I really look like?"*

Regardless of what you saw, there's a good chance you'd like to improve it. What changes would you like to make?

Answering the question of how you want to look is more complicated than you might think. As I have said all along, it's essential to know where you want to go - what financial success means to YOU - to make a real plan for achieving those goals. Before you can make a workable plan, however, you must know where you want to go.

Many people make the mistake of simply thinking that if they had more money, their lives would be better. They don't stop to think about the specifics such as how MUCH more, nor do they think about what changes they're willing to make to achieve wealth. But without knowing these things, it's impossible to figure out how to get to where you want to go.

Just imagine if I gave you $1 more than you're earning right now. That's technically more money, right! What you must do is allow yourself to be specific about what you truly want in life. The more definitive you are about what you do want, the easier it is for the *"Universe"* to give it to you.

Remember the Genie in Aladdin: *"Your wish is my command."* It's time to get specific about what you do want to achieve in your life.

The Vehicle Analogy

Disclaimer: Most *"Cars"* depreciate over time; therefore, they do not fall under the true sense of being an Investment Vehicle and as such, I do not recommend them as a Wealth Creation Strategy.

Let me float an idea with you if I may, that I believe most people can relate to. I want you, for this analogy, to think of investment vehicles, (i.e. property, shares or businesses), as if they were used cars.

Now imagine going onto a used car lot and seeing a "red" sports car (remembering that most people believe red cars go faster.) The used car salesman (the so-called wealth guru) tells you how the car worked for the previous owner (usually themselves) and what it can achieve for you if you were to buy it.

But what you may not know is the car was driven in a different environment, on different roads, by a driver with a different purpose in life and different skills and beliefs to you.

And just because it performed well for the previous driver, there's no guarantee it will perform to the same standards for you (a point that's rarely made mention of.)

You also need to take into consideration: how many kilometers are on the clock, wear and tear on the engine and bodywork, has it been in any previous accidents (some so-called wealth gurus tout that they have gone bankrupt 2-3 times in their lives before making it big – were they driving this vehicle when that happened? Did they then join the original vehicle with another to create what you see in front of you now?

So, let me ask you some questions: Do you like , for example, *"Fords"* because your Father loved them? Is a *"Ford"* the best car for you and your specific needs? What are you teaching your kids to drive in? Why are you only teaching them in one brand of car?

Some people continually upgrade their current vehicle to the latest model, knowing that it is not giving them the satisfaction that they crave. However, they are too concerned with what others will say if they were to move away from that make of vehicle to test drive something different. Something that is clearly more suitable to their current and future needs. And which will help them to achieve their perfect life.

Does this sound like someone you know? Or does it sound like you at some point in your life?

Without knowing what you want to achieve in your life and the direction you need to be traveling, any vehicle is as good as the next. It just means you'll be taking the *"scenic route"* through your life.

Now don't get me wrong. I love to stop, take in the view and smell the flowers along my journey. And I also know my destination will provide me with the abundance of all the flowers and magnificent things in life that I want.

So, without knowing the end purpose or the road you will be traveling along, answer this question: *"What's the 'best vehicle' you can buy?"*

What answer popped into your head?

- Was it some sort of expensive sports car such as a Porsche, Maserati, or Lamborghini or even a convertible?

- Was it a luxury sedan such as a Mercedes, BMW, or Lexus?

- Maybe it was a highly fuel-efficient hybrid or an affordable midsize.

- Was it a tough 4-wheel drive such as a Jeep or a Hummer?

- What about a hefty truck?

- Or even a motorcycle – road or off-road?

Clearly, a few clarifying questions of your own would help you come up with a better answer. In fact, your first answer might appear ridiculous once you get the full picture. Further helpful information would include, but is certainly not limited to:

- Roads… Will it be driven on quality highways with pavement in great condition? Or will it be driven on mountainous tracks loaded with potholes and mud?

- Personal... Is it for one or two people. Or will you need to transport a family?

- Fuel… Will fuel be easily available. Or will you need to travel far distances between re-fueling points?

- Cargo… Do you need to carry cargo or tow a trailer?

The list could go on, but you get the point. Without knowing the vehicle's purpose, the question is impossible to answer correctly. You might, through sheer luck, have picked a vehicle that's great for its intended use. However, you might also have picked something that's totally wrong for the job.

Applying this vehicle analogy to your finances works in a similar way. If you don't think about the purpose of money in your life, your chances of being happy with your financial situation are slim. If you don't clarify the specifics of your financial goals, you're unlikely to choose the best investment vehicle to get you to where you want to go.

There are thousands of potential investments, just as there are thousands of cars available for purchase. Decisions about which to invest in should be based on your personal characteristics, circumstances and financial goals. Just because someone else has taken a particular path to wealth doesn't mean it will work for you.

In fact, it's helpful to think of your plan for wealth in three phases:

1. *Decide Where You Want To Go:* Define what financial success looks like to YOU. What does success look like to YOU? How do you want your image in *The Money Mirror* to look?

2. *Pick A Path:* Identify the types of investments and strategies that are most likely to move you toward your goals. What can you do to change your money image so that it's closer to your ideal? Start to find mentors who will speed up your journey.

3.   *Take The First Steps:* Once you know where you want to go and how you think you can get there, you can begin to take steps. What specific things can you do to begin to change your money image?

Let's begin by focusing on the first of these three phases: deciding where you want to go. Deciding where you're going can be difficult, because it's rarely as simple as deciding to *"become wealthy."* What is wealth? How much is enough? What tradeoffs are you willing to make to get there, such as giving up free time to increase income?

You've already imagined what your perfect life looks like. Now it's time to get more specific.

Thinking Beyond The Numbers

Remember the old saying, *"money can't buy you happiness?"* Well, you don't have to look far to see this is true. Examples of wealthy people who are unhappy are everywhere.

Consider the number of rich (and famous) movie stars, musicians, sportsmen and women and others whose money doesn't seem to be making them happy. Many are addicted to alcohol or drugs and find themselves in and out of rehabilitation programs. Lasting marriages and relationships are relatively rare. Some people even become suicidal.

In the richest of families, where children may be wildly wealthy simply by being born into the family, similar struggles are often chronicled in the newspapers and on television.

This is not to say having money is not a worthy goal. But it is important to understand its proper role in life. Happiness won't follow from a simple accumulation of a large balance in your bank account.

Just because you have a million dollars in the bank doesn't mean you'll suddenly feel differently. Now, if reaching the million-dollar mark represents an achievement of one of your essential goals, it may bring you enormous satisfaction.

My point is, the numbers on a piece of paper may not be enough to make you feel successful or happy.

You may be thinking I'm crazy here. After all, if you had a million dollars in the bank, you might think that would be enough to make you wildly happy. But money is simply a magnifier of the person you were before you had it. Let me give you an example:

Sam and Leah worked very hard. They saved a lot of money. They made wise investments. And over the years, their money grew. Life went on. Children, houses, cars, and increasingly stressful jobs. Their lifestyle became more expensive as they moved through life. Bigger bills, school fees, and other expenses increased as their incomes rose.

Sam tried to keep up with their investments regularly. But as busy as life was, he only put together all the necessary information occasionally. One day, he added up the figures and found their assets totaled over a million dollars. He felt a momentary spurt of excitement and went in to tell Leah. However, Leah was busy with cooking a meal, and the youngest child needed help in the bath. Life went on and the excitement faded.

Sam and Leah carried on as before, working and saving. They didn't celebrate the achievement of their goal because the million dollars was just a number. Yes, granted a nice number, with several zeros at the end. But it was just a number. It didn't represent the achievement of their goal. Because Sam and Leah didn't really have goals (other than to keep saving.)

They had never really thought about what financial success was to them or how / why they would achieve it. They just kept working and saving and working and saving. Without any other goals or dreams to attach to the number 1,000,000, it's just another number.

Regardless of the number you choose, there's always a number higher. For Sam, he looked at a million and thought about reaching two million. So, how much is enough? If you haven't thought that through, NO amount is enough. Each number is just a number.

Now think about this differently. What if you had defined success to include several goals and one of them was to pay off your home? What if, for you, having no debt on your home implied happiness, security and a legacy for your children?

So, imagine the amount of the loan on your home is $300,000. And eliminating that debt is a crucial part of your picture of financial success. Think about paying down the loan amount over time. Picture yourself on the day you make the final payment and the loan balance goes to $0. You've reached your goal! You've achieved an important part of your dream of success! You celebrate!

Here's another way to think about this. If owning your home (free of debt) is part of your definition of financial success, it'll help you make better decisions about how much to spend on a house. Would you be happier in a smaller house that is totally paid for? Or in a larger house where you still have a loan?

There's no *"right"* answer. You might have one opinion and I might have another.

And that's why it's so important to think about YOUR perfect life. The word *"life"* is important here, too. Sam and Leah didn't think in terms of *"life"* and a number on a piece of paper left them with little to celebrate.

Wealth As A Tool

A concept related to thinking beyond the numbers is the idea that wealth is a tool. Money, in and of itself, brings little happiness. It's just paper or numbers on a computer screen. And it brings little joy to most people.

Obviously, it's the things you can DO with money that make it integral to happiness. For each person, the best use of money may vary. I may gain the most satisfaction from spending my money on things that aren't important to you. You may think it's important to use your wealth in ways that don't appeal to me.

The essential point is that money is a TOOL. It's a convenient way to keep score in the *"Game of Life."* You gain satisfaction from how you use it, even if that use is to save for your future security.

So, as you begin to think of what financial success looks like to you. It's important to go beyond the number in the bank and think about the things you'd like to be able to do with that money. Meeting such goals feels much more real.

Sticking to a financial plan is far easier when you've visualized a LIFE rather than a number.

Never get so busy making a living
that you forget to make a life

\- Anonymous

Defining Your Idea Of Success

What do you want to see when you look in *The Money Mirror*? What you see should be whatever is needed to provide you with the life you want. Go back to your thoughts in Chapter 1 about your perfect life. Chances are, you were general. Now let's get to some specific goals.

Think about your perfect day. Visualize it in detail.

Here are some things you should consider; some will be more or less important to you and you'll certainly have other priorities on your own list.

- How would you spend your time?

- What would you do immediately when you got up? Then what?

- Would you be working? Working in an office? Working for someone else? Self-employed? Working from home?

- How much would you be working? All day? Only part of the day?

- How would you be spending the time you weren't working? Traveling? Gardening? Reading? Entertaining? Exercising? Hobbies? Visiting friends or family?

- Where would you live? What town or neighborhood? What country?

- What would your house look like? Outside? Inside? Would you have more than one?

- What would you be driving?

- What would you be wearing?

- What would you look like? What sort of health are you in?

- In your perfect life, when you think about money, what will you feel?

- What past financial obligations would be taken care of completely? What debts would be paid for in full? Your house? Everything?

- What future financial obligations would be taken care of completely? Would your retirement be secure? Your children's education paid for?

Think about these and other areas in your life that are important to you. Remember to free yourself from negative or limiting thoughts and beliefs.

Because, this is YOUR perfect life if there were no money-related issues. This is YOUR perfect life if you knew you could achieve absolutely anything.

Napoleon Hill said it best when he said...

What the mind can conceive
and believe, it will achieve!

Putting A Price On Perfection

Once you have a list of the specific things that together comprise your perfect life, you can begin to put a price on them. You can use resources, such as real estate advertising or the internet, to get an idea of what your perfect house would cost. You can also put a price on many other things in this way.

You will also know the amounts you currently owe from your financial snapshot. If your perfect life means that these debts go away, you can easily put a price on that.

Some parts of your perfect life may require more work. For example, if you want to have your children's education paid for completely, you'll need to estimate how much money it would take.

It's also likely that when you really sit down and think about it, some of what is in your perfect life doesn't involve money at all. For example, if part of *"perfect"* for you is that you spend more time reading, your path to happiness may also include an element of how to better use your time.

However, it may be that finding time for yourself comes down to financial issues such as building enough wealth to be able to hire someone to take care of some of your home tasks so that you can have more time to do other things.

As noted, wealth is a tool that can be very useful in getting you where you want to go. Not having enough money or having money worries can clearly lead to unhappiness. Another part of this thought process is deciding which things are most essential to your happiness. If you work toward those first through your priorities, you will be making faster strides toward your ultimate goals.

Priorities

Even in your perfect life, you may need to make choices. There are only 24 hours in each day, for example. So, you may not be able to do everything you want to do every day.

You may also decide that some pieces of your perfect life are worth giving up for the sake of others. Start to think about what things are your top priorities. If you had to put them in order of the ones that are most important to you, how would they look?

For example, is it more important to work less (if that is one of your goals), or drive an expensive car? Would you give up your dream of a big house in an upscale neighborhood if it meant you could spend more time pursuing your hobbies?

Some priorities are easy to see. If you owe money on your home, for instance, the loan involves a set timeline for repayment. You can make it a goal to pay it down faster, of course. Or decide the house isn't worth it to you and choose to sell. However, repayment of existing debts should, at a minimum, occur on time.

Other priorities are difficult to measure. Would you be happier in a tiny house that's paid for and easy to take care of if it allowed you to spend more time and money traveling? Would you rather live more frugally now and retire sooner? Only you can decide the answers to such questions.

Choosing priorities is NOT the same as assuming you can't reach your goals. It also doesn't have to mean you're thinking negative thoughts or giving up on your dreams.

However, it's often preferable to identify the areas that are particularly bothersome and take care of them first. Which piece of your financial image is the one that causes you the most problems? Is it a particular debt? A need not met that is really destroying your happiness? It only makes sense to take care of those first. Given time, you can deal with the rest.

Sometimes, you will want to change the timing of your spending and saving to meet needs. You may decide an expenditure you thought was essential is less important than something else. Perhaps you'd prefer to simplify your life and find a path to wealth that way.

In short, having it all is not a guarantee of happiness. Think of your wealth as a tool to use wisely. You may find you can make a significant difference in your life quickly. Partly through better use of your money and partly because of a change in your attitude.

Money gives you choices! …And choices give you FREEDOM!

Don't Rush Your Definition Of Perfection

You may need to take a few days thinking about your perfect life. Find some time away from your daily stresses. Think deeply about what really matters most to you.

It may be helpful to put yourself back in the mindset you had as a child. What was important to you back then? What did you dream of doing when you were older? What did it take to make you happy and what was a perfect day for you? Can this help you define your perfect life now?

It's natural for your goals to change over time. Sometimes, this is for the better, but sometimes it's for the worse. The essential thing is to really get to what drives your happiness, and then think of the role money can play.

Many of the same factors that can keep you from seeing your financial situation clearly can keep you from understanding what your perfect life is. Your past experiences influence your first responses to the question of what your perfect life looks like. You may have to clear your mind of impressions going back to your childhood about what you *"should"* do and how your life *"should"* look.

Your parents' choices and their attitudes toward money and work in your house when you were young certainly play a role in your thoughts about those topics today.

Similarly, your personality and your mood can shape your perception of what you want. Be careful of defining your perfect life based on such things. Moods change, and your personality may influence your decisions about your financial future and goals.

Any limiting beliefs you hold have the potential to alter your thoughts about what is possible. They can affect your definition of your perfect life and how big your dreams are. I want to encourage you again to be aware of how limitations in your belief in yourself can cause you to keep your goals too conservative.

This is the time to dream big! What have you always wanted? You can find deep and lasting happiness and money can help you get there. Don't sell yourself short by defining your perfect life to be less than it can be.

Love him or loath him, there is no denying Donald Trump sums it up best when he says...

If you're going to think anything,
it may as well be BIG!

I like to take this concept one step further and think... HUGE!

Once you have defined Your *"perfect life,"* sit with that picture for a while. Think about the specifics of what it means. Consider how your days would look. Don't be distracted by what anyone else might or might not agree with. Remember, it's Your Perfect Life you're creating.

When you're good and comfortable with your vision of where you want to go, fix it firmly in your mind. Make your perfect life as real and as vivid to you as your current life. Start behaving as if you're already there. Never lose sight of your perfect life. Keep it close to you as encouragement and validation of your path. Believe in it and believe in yourself.

With the right mindset and a workable plan, you can achieve great things. So how do you get to a workable plan? You know where you're going (your perfect life) and you know where you are (your financial snapshot.) What's left is to connect the dots.

Comparing Your Current Situation To Your Perfect Life

Once you identify your perfect life, you can begin to visualize where you want to go. Compare this image to your current financial snapshot. How far off is it?

Where are the biggest problem areas? Too much debt? Not enough security? Can't afford to buy the things you need to live a satisfying life? Rising expenses? Too little income? All of these?

For Further Thought:

Are You Happy With What You See?

1. In this chapter, you thought about your perfect life. If you're like most of us, the first time you thought about what your perfect life looked like, it was rather different from what you decided on after you thought a little longer. How did your definition of your perfect life change the longer you thought about it?

   _____

   _____

   _____

   _____

   _____

2. What could have kept you (or still be keeping you) from seeing your perfect life clearly? (Examples: expectations of others, past experiences.)

   _____

   _____

   _____

   _____

   _____

   _____

3. Do you feel confident that the way you now view your perfect life is the true expression of your inner desires and dreams? If Not, why not? (Remember there is always room for fine tuning and tweaking.)

_____

_____

_____

_____

4.   Many elements of your perfect life can be broken down into specific goal elements such as owning a house. Others can be defined in money terms, such as paying off a debt. Use the table below to define the pieces of your perfect life that involve a specific cost. An example row has been completed for you.

Goal Element	**Cost Estimate**
Own a 4-bedroom home in a Coastal View neighborhood.	$500,000
TOTAL	

5.   Some pieces of your perfect life may not be specific things you can purchase or pay for. What aspects of your perfect life don't really fit in a table like the one above? (For example, if one goal is to spend more time with your family or friends, you may not be able to quantify that into a direct dollar figure.)

_____

_____

_____

_____

_____

_____

_____

6.   How can you use money as a tool to achieve those less-specific parts of your perfect life?

_____

_____

_____

_____

_____

_____

_____

_____

_____

_____

*If you don't want to write in your book… You can download all the exercises at:
www.TheMoneyMirrorBook.com/resources

Rae Brent

Chapter 7

Finding The Path To Your Perfect Life

N ow let's start to uncover ways you can take control of your finances, begin to change what is reflected in your *Money Mirror,* and find a path to your perfect life.

We'll also look at several areas that are potential obstacles to your financial success such as your job, knowledge, education, habits, and others.

Previously, you asked yourself these questions based on your current financial snapshot:

- Arc you happy and encouraged by what you see? Do you feel comfortable with where you stand? Is it better or worse than you expected?

- Is the total amount you own larger than the total amount you owe?

- Is the total coming in larger than the total going out?

You also developed a clear vision of your perfect life. Including estimating the amount of money you will require to achieve your financial goals.

So how do you get from where you are to where you want to be?

By starting with the key principle. You need to have more money coming in than you have going out.

No matter what else you do, if you continually spend more than you earn, you will never achieve your perfect life. Overspending leads to increasing debt. It leaves nothing to invest in your future. It leads to an out-of-control financial situation.

There are only two ways to eliminate overspending:

- Increase income, or

- Decrease expenses.

It's amazing how many people seem to forget this very simple truth. They work through budgets and assumptions and calculations and so on, but they never get to the point where their income exceeds their expenses.

You can change your financial image by re-aligning these two variables. The larger the gap between your income and your expenses, the faster your image will begin to change.

Once your income exceeds your expenses, you can begin to make real progress paying down your debts and investing in your future. Your wealth will begin to work for you. It will begin to sustain itself, and you can move closer to your perfect life.

Let's look first at how to increase your income.

Increasing Income

Sometimes, increasing income requires less effort than expected. Many of us fall into a trap of just accepting what we get and moving through life. We don't seek out new ways to make more money. But sit and wait for the raise the boss might offer or the new job someone might call us about.

There are many reasons for this inertia and breaking free of these tendencies can be very rewarding. Here are some strategies for bumping up your income.

Start With Your Current Sources Of Income

You have already put together information on your income in your financial snapshot. Let's take another look at that information.

What are your sources of income? For many people, there is only one source: their primary job. If you happen to have Multiple Sources of Income (MSIs), that's great news.

Working for someone else is the most common means of earning a living. Companies often have policies of offering annual cost-of-living adjustments, and many employees never ask for anything beyond that amount.

However, it is possible that you're able to ask for a salary increase more than this small annual increase. The first step is to gather some research to support your request.

Search the Internet, library, or newspaper for jobs like yours. Look at the salary ranges offered. How does yours compare? Given your level of experience, are you underpaid compared to the going rate? Is there evidence that there are a lot of jobs for people with your skill set? If so, you may be able to ask for a salary increase.

Assuming your job performance has been adequate, if you can find evidence that you're paid below the typical wage, consider asking for an increase. If your job performance has been outstanding, you're in an even better position.

Each employer-employee relationship is different. There is no guarantee that your boss would be willing or able to grant you a salary / wage increase. However, there is little risk in asking, particularly if you prepare yourself with evidence such as:

- Higher pay offered for jobs like yours,

- Strong job performance (particularly if you can document increasing the company's income or decreasing its expenses), and

- Demand for people with your set of skills in the workforce.

Your employer has little incentive to offer you extra money if you don't ask. They are in business to make money, and if you appear to be satisfied where you are, why would they offer more? Don't assume the answer would be *"No"* before you ask the question.

The answer will be *"No"* 100% of the time if you don't ASK! Because, you have to A-S-K to G-E-T!

Of course, some judgment must be exercised here. Ultimatums are always a bad idea, and you don't want to back your employer into a corner. However, if you have been doing a good job and can demonstrate that you may be underpaid, by the job markets standards, you may find your boss stepping up with a pay increase if you'll only ask.

Look For Other Sources Of Income

There are significant benefits to having Multiple Streams of Income (MSIs.) If you rely on only one source of income, you have some additional vulnerability to situations such as layoffs or other cutbacks. If you receive income from various sources, it's unlikely that you would lose all of them at the same time. It's also possible to increase your total income well beyond your primary job's pay.

So how do you begin to find other sources of income? The first thing you must do is begin to open your mind to the idea. Chances are you've come across some means of earning extra cash over the past few months. If you weren't receptive to the thought of other ways to earn income, however, you may have missed them entirely.

I once read a story about a family who began a small garden patch in one corner of their yard. At first, they just grew the typical fruits and vegetables a household would eat. Over time and as their gardening skills improved, they began selling some of the extra produce at the local market. The garden plot grew, and the family figured out which crops took up the least space and offered the highest profit margins.

The income from the garden expanded, and within a few years, it became a significant source of additional money. The nice thing about this was that it really didn't require all that much extra work. A weekly trip down to the market and a little extra work were needed, but not a full-time or cash-intensive commitment. The family used the money to pay down debt and then began an investing program. The resulting addition to their wealth will be substantial.

Do you have a marketable skill you could use to generate extra money? People pay a lot for services ranging from home repairs to lawn care. It's a good idea to check your contract or policies at your primary job before embarking on any secondary earnings effort. Some companies prohibit such activities, particularly if they are like your job.

There are many ways to earn extra income. Some require a large investment of time or money; others are less involved. Potential earnings also vary.

As you begin to seek out these additional income streams, it is important to proceed with some caution. Any *"opportunity"* that seems too good to be true should be thoroughly researched to ensure that it's legitimate. There are unscrupulous individuals and companies around the world that are quick to take your money and slow to offer you any real potential for earnings.

A quick Internet search may be sufficient to tell you a firm is plagued with a bad reputation, for example. Various agencies such as the Better Business Bureau in the US or A.S.I.C. in Australia log reports of improper activities and can be good sources of information about a company's reputation.

As you begin to work to change your financial image, it is likely that opportunities will begin to present themselves. Keep your mind open to them and be prepared to take advantage of those that offer good potential for you.

The Other Side Of The Equation: Expenses

Obviously, the other way to make your income exceed your expenses is to reduce your expenses. It's helpful to begin to change your mindset about spending even before you get to the nuts and bolts.

Many of us fall into the trap of spending for things that really don't bring us happiness. How many times have you made a purchase only to discover that you really didn't need or want the thing you spent your hard-earned cash on? Expenses can quickly get out of control. Even worse, many times purchases are made on credit, and interest charges and fees can spiral in no time at all.

Before you even begin to budget or plan for future expenses, it's important to think about how your spending is related to your happiness. You probably have some expenses that are beyond your control (at least over a short period of time) such as your rent or house payment. Even if you could move and potentially reduce this spending, it would probably take some time.

However, there are other expenses that are purely a choice such as the coffee you buy on the way to your office, the clothes you purchase over the weekend, the dinner out you enjoy each week, or whatever it is that you spend your money to buy. Overdoing it for these things can push your financial situation out of control in a hurry.

Begin to think about the link between these things and your happiness. If you are feeling the pinch of too much debt, I'll bet you'd feel much more relaxed if you'd stop the spending and reduce the debt.

Even the items you can't change right away, such as your housing or your car, you can shift given time. If your house is just too expensive for you to comfortably afford right now, you might increase your overall happiness by selling it and moving into something less pricey.

No budget can be successful if you have an unhealthy attitude toward spending. Stop and think about why you spend what you do. What were your most recent purchases? Did they bring you joy when you bought them? Do they still?

Begin to think about your triggers for spending. Is it to please someone else? Are you trying to impress someone? Do you spend when you're upset about something? Do you give in to impulses?

Spending money you can afford to spend for things you really want is certainly a pleasure. However, the same cannot be said if the purchase overextends your budget. Even if your income is growing, if your spending is growing faster, you're moving backwards.

Blocks To Success

There are several things that can be blocks to success. It's important to understand these and how they may apply to you. While there are others, the most common blocks to financial success include:

- A lack of control of your finances,
- Your job and sources of income,
- Your knowledge (or lack of knowledge),
- Your education or training level,
- Your beliefs about yourself and your potential,
- Your habits, and
- Your commitment to change.

Each of these can slow or stop your progress toward your perfect life. It's important to think about how these and other aspects of your personality, choices, or lifestyle could be keeping you from reaching your financial (and life) goals.

Lack Of Control

John and Susan are a busy couple with two lovely children. They both work and have good incomes. While they aren't extravagant, they do enjoy spending the money they work so hard to earn. They live in a nice house and drive relatively new cars. The children, two girls, are always dressed in the latest pre-teen fashions and have the latest electronic gadgets.

Proud of the fact that they pay off most of their credit card balances every month, John and Susan are nonetheless becoming concerned about the fact that they haven't yet begun to save for their retirement or the girls' college education. John's theory is they'll save once their incomes grow larger. He's expecting a raise in a few months, and Susan's job is also going well. Not 20 minutes later, he mentioned the larger house they're eyeing in a more expensive neighborhood.

John has missed a crucial point. While their income is rising, so are their expenses. Unless John and Susan take control, they are unlikely to get ahead or ever build real wealth.

Bob Proctor has explained this relationship by describing three types of people (or families.) The first type is the one where spending exceeds income. Debts grow, and financial dreams grow further away instead of closer. The second type of person spends basically everything they make. While they may not be going backwards, neither are they moving ahead. The third type of people do save and build wealth because their spending is less than their income.

Bob points out that it is wrong to assume that as your income rises, you'll naturally move from one category to the next. Instead, those who habitually overspend are likely to continue to overspend even as their income rises. I believe Bob is right.

The only way to escape this truth is to take control. You must decide what financial success means to you, make a good plan, and stick to it even if you must change your current patterns.

John and Susan will never build real wealth unless they take charge of their financial situation. They're fortunate enough to be starting from a relatively comfortable position. But if they don't stop and think where they're going and how they want to get there, they may begin to go backwards. As retirement begins to loom, they may be forced to drastically change their lifestyle or face huge future problems. If they want to help their children with their education, they should start saving now.

Are you like John and Susan? Are you just moving through your financial life without a firm grip? If so, I hope you've already visualized your perfect life and begun to realize what you'll need to do to reach that goal. By reading this book, you've already begun to take control.

Your Job And Sources Of Income

Another block to success can be your job and other sources of income. We talked about how you might be able to improve your current earnings from your job, as well as the potential for other sources of income.

However, some jobs can become insurmountable blocks to financial success. They can keep you from achieving the life you want to lead in several ways. Some of these are obvious, but others are less so.

Jobs that pay too little can be a block to your perfect life. There are people who work and work but bring home very little income. While it is possible to survive on very little in the way of income, some people with very low incomes can (and do) build wealth. But there's no doubt a job that pays poorly makes it more difficult.

You may feel stuck in the job you're in due to your level of skills / education / training or other issues. However, this is certainly worth confirming. I have seen very intelligent people stay with jobs out of habit or fear even though they could have done far better in other places.

It is also possible that even a relatively high-paying job can be a block to reaching your goals. If your perfect life, for example, includes working less and that would be difficult in your current job, you may face a difficult choice.

Similarly, some people settle for good jobs and incomes when they could have had GREAT ones if they'd only been willing to take a risk. Many times, jobs that pay well involve long hours, stress, travel, or other commitments. These can absorb your energy and hinder your creativity.

Even a good salary may be keeping you from your perfect life. Are you overstressed? Overworked? Unfulfilled? Even if your paycheck is large, it's worth analyzing whether you might be happier in a different position.

A friend of mine graduated from a prestigious university in the US with a business degree. He went to work in a bank and was doing very well. He was good at his job and his salary was high and rising. However, he hated every minute of it. He found the work dull and dry and boring. One day, with the full support of his wife, he handed in his letter of resignation and bought a small company.

Now, he can see the fruits of his labor directly even though his high-priced degree is little more than a piece of paper on the wall. While there were some rather difficult years, his company continues to grow and will one day be worth a substantial amount. When it sells, he will have reached his financial goals in a way I don't think the bank would ever have enabled him to do. He's also enjoyed life along the way.

Your other sources of income (or lack thereof) can also be blocks. If you don't develop MSIs, you're vulnerable to the success or failure of one company. You also limit yourself to the earning potential of one job.

Don't assume adding a source of income implies a large commitment of time. There are strategies to add income through using your creativity and resources that don't always involve an ongoing need for a large amount of time.

As I mentioned in the introduction to this book, I have always been interested in real estate investments. From just a few properties years ago to a portfolio of many today, I have assembled a portfolio which is now earning a substantial income. While I certainly must keep an eye on these investments to ensure they are maintained and rented, I don't spend all day every day at each location.

In fact, I can pursue several other opportunities at the same time. The rental incomes keep coming in month after month. By following my own interest in real estate, I've added a significant income.

Another word of caution is appropriate here. There are get-rich-quick schemes in real estate just as there are in many other areas. Unscrupulous people will advise you to invest in assets that are way overpriced or will never turn a profit. As always, a healthy dose of common sense is warranted including carrying out your own research which is referred to as *"Due Diligence."*

Remember also, to listen to your intuition, or *"gut feelings"* as some people refer to them. So, if it *"doesn't feel / look / sound right,"* question / investigate the opportunity further or just walk away from it.

Your Knowledge (Or Lack Of Knowledge)

Knowledge limitations can be another block to your success. Without the knowledge needed to be a good manager of your finances, for example, you are more likely to make mistakes. If you lack the information about an area you're thinking of investing in, you're more likely to choose poorly.

The resources available today to gain knowledge and information are amazing. There are classes and books and magazines and websites. You can search the Internet for any topic and download a wealth of information. I have listed some of my own favorite resources at the end of this book.

But, before you pursue any investment. It's wise to accumulate enough knowledge to ensure you aren't being taken in by a shiny appearance with little underlying value. Start by reading financial magazines. Regularly visit good financial websites. Before you know it, you'll begin to build a base of knowledge that will help you reach your goals.

Your Education Or Training Level

While education and training are not magic answers to the question of how to grow wealthy, they can certainly be helpful. There are many examples of people who have been extremely successful without much in the way of formal education or training. However, for most of us, a good background of education or some quality training can be very valuable for opening the doors to opportunities. A lack of such a background, for example, can be a block to finding a better paying job.

It's essential that any training or education you pursue is in alignment with your vision of your perfect life. While there may be intrinsic value to education, it doesn't always translate into more money. Moreover, if it prepares you to do something that doesn't fit your goals, it's not moving you down the right path.

I have seen first-hand the working of this in my own life. After my military career, I moved in several directions. I was like a kid in a candy store until I became definitive about what I wanted to see in my *Money Mirror*. I finally discovered marketing / copywriting. And I knew I had found the training I wanted to pursue. Over the past several years, I've attended conferences and seminars which have greatly expanded my knowledge and skills in these areas. Many of them were in the USA (half a world away.)

I'm certainly not advocating marketing / copywriting is for everyone. My point is I found the perfect fit for me. And with an open mind and an eye toward your perfect life, you can also find the education or training you need to move you down the path toward your perfect life.

A lack of education can be a tough obstacle to get around. Without skills or training that has value in the job market, it's difficult to make progress. Higher incomes tend to be correlated with greater levels of education. This doesn't always mean several years at a university; it may be that a night class or specialized training is the better course of action for you. Webinars are great for this too. Although you may find yourself getting up in the middle of the night to attend them.

Investing in yourself in the right direction for YOU can be a major factor in how quickly you achieve your perfect life.

Finding a Mentor will propel you forward at great speeds. All successful people have mentors for different aspects of their lives. Find people who are *"walking their talk"* in the areas you're interested in. This has certainly made the difference in my life. By knowing what you want out of life, you are then able to search out the appropriate people who are already successful in that field to be a mentor to you.

Remember… *"Success Leaves Clues!"* So, be prepared to seek them out and hire them. At the end of the day, you aren't paying them… you're investing in yourself!

Your Beliefs About Yourself And Your Potential

The beliefs you have about yourself are a huge factor in relation to your success. Limiting beliefs are one of the few blocks that can be insurmountable if not dealt with. If you lack the belief in your power to succeed and achieve your goals, it will be extremely difficult to reach your perfect life.

Your Habits

Your habits can also be blocking your success. These can be little things or larger problems. When you looked at your financial snapshot, you may have seen some signs of these. Some habits involve spending without thinking or purchasing items that really aren't important to you. You may also lack good habits such as saving.

Without a doubt, you can fall into the habit of spending without thinking. Even something as simple as the habit of stopping into the coffee shop for a latte on your way to work can add up.

Do the math and you'll see that on a monthly basis, it can turn into real money. Little luxuries such as a coffee house treat can be an important part of enjoying your day. But sometimes it's more of a habit than anything. How much would you miss it if you went for the regular cup of coffee Monday through Thursday and the expensive cappuccino or latte on Fridays? You might find you enjoy your once-a-week treat more than the everyday routine.

There are many other bad habits that can cost you money over time. Here are just a few examples:

- Not paying off credit cards every month and incurring finance and / or late charges,

- Impulse purchasing, particularly for big-ticket items (without proper research or waiting to see that it's really something you want), or

- Smoking, eating out, and other expensive habits.

Clearly, this list could go on for pages and pages. The point is, any habit that leads you to spend more money WITHOUT adding sufficiently to the quality of your life can be a huge block to your success. What joy do you receive from incurring interest charges on your credit cards? NONE!

Your Commitment To Change

Unless you commit to making the appropriate changes in your day to day life, nothing will change to move you forward to achieving your perfect life.

Decide – Commit – Act

Once you have decided that you want to change, make a commitment to yourself to change and then take some appropriate action towards making those changes. No one else will make the changes in your life for you. You are responsible for the life you are creating. If you don't like where you currently are, then decide – commit – act to implement changes.

The list of potential blocks could go on; each of us has our own set of challenges. Some of these are more difficult to change than others, but you should not fall into the trap of assuming you can't change your financial image.

Again, with sufficient will and a workable plan, virtually every aspect of your financial picture can be altered over time.

For Further Thought:

Finding The Path To Your Perfect Life

1. As you visualize your perfect life and compare it to your current life, what things stand out as the most pressing to change to enable you to begin to live your perfect life?

    _____
    _____
    _____
    _____
    _____

2. Are you able to ask for a pay increase at your primary job? If so, what points would you raise in a conversation with your boss?

    _____
    _____
    _____
    _____
    _____
    _____

3. Begin to think about potential ways to secure additional streams of income. Think about ideas and jot them down as they come to you. What are some things you are good at or enjoy doing?

    _____
    _____
    _____
    _____

4. What habits can you think of that cost you money but don't bring you the satisfaction in the life you desire?

_____

_____

_____

_____

_____

_____

5. What do you see as the biggest blocks to reaching your perfect life?

_____

_____

_____

_____

_____

_____

6. What course(s) of action could you consider eliminating these blocks? (Example: attend a training class, read a book, find a mentor, etc.)

_____

_____

_____

_____

_____

_____

*If you don't want to write in your book... You can download all the exercises at:
www.TheMoneyMirrorBook.com/resources

Rae Brent

Chapter 8

Making A Plan To Change Your Financial Image

L et me introduce you to a saying I have taken to heart from my days in the Army. It's called... *The 7 'P's*, and it goes like this...

Prior Preparation and Planning...
Prevents Piss Poor Performance!

So far, you've looked at your finances through *The Money Mirror*; that is a snapshot of where you are now. You've also thought about your perfect life, which is where you want to be. We then looked at potential paths to take you from where you are to where you want to go.

The success of any planning effort is dependent on these steps. If you know where you're going and the ways you want to get there, it's far easier to plan the specifics. Moreover, if you don't have a firm grasp on what you're attempting to achieve and what's important to you in the process of achieving it, your chances for success are unfortunately small.

Think of it like planning a vacation. First, you must know where you're going. Then you decide how you're going to travel there. Then you deal with the details, book your flight, pack your suitcase, and take off.

Obviously, you can't pack your suitcase if you don't know where you're going: do you need snow gear or swimsuits? Similarly, you can't make a good financial plan if you don't have a clear picture of what you're attempting to achieve.

Even if you've made financial plans in the past, if they only dealt with specifics, they were probably almost impossible to stick with over a long period of time. Similarly, if you just picked up a budget or plan from somewhere else (such as a financial advisor or money-oriented website or elsewhere) and tried to use it, it probably didn't work either unless it happened to fit your goals.

It can be very difficult to keep spending under control. In our society, marketing images tempt us nonstop with products and services. It's all too easy to spend, spend, spend! As discussed earlier, our belief systems can also leave us with tendencies to want to acquire things or purchase them for others. In fact, overspending is one of the primary reasons people end up with out-of-control finances and money-related unhappiness.

For these reasons and many others, making a financial plan and sticking to a budget can be very difficult. If you are having negative thoughts right now, consider why that might be. Have you tried to budget in the past and failed? Does the word "budget" make you think of depriving yourself and being unhappy? Are your limiting beliefs playing a role?

I encourage you to think about it differently. Living within a budget can be very liberating. In fact, living within a budget is one of the most important things you can do to stop money problems from making you unhappy. By taking control of your finances in this very tangible way, you can begin to move down your path toward your perfect life.

Don't let the idea of a budget become a negative thought for you. A budget is just a tool to be sure you get the maximum enjoyment from your money. By budgeting, you determine where your income is spent. You decide how you want your financial picture to look, and you use a budget to help you get there.

Even if you've attempted budgeting previously with little success, it's a very different process when you combine it with your own definition of success and your perfect life.

How To Make A Plan Based On Your Definition Of Financial Success

As I've said throughout this book, unless you look inside yourself to identify YOUR financial goals and definition of success, you undermine your chances of ever reaching your perfect life. So, once you've defined your financial success, how do you get there?

A general mindset towards the wise use of money (spending less than your income, for example) is a precursor to an effective plan. Once you have reached a point of understanding the path you want to take to improve your financial situation, it's time to get specific.

Your definition of financial success is integral to this planning process. While all plans have common characteristics, there are also areas where your preferences and goals play a role in determining the specifics. Depending on your goals, your plan may take different shapes. Here are a few examples.

Janet wants to be able to quit her job and start a new company. She has several credit card bills that need to be paid. She also needs to put away enough money to pay her living expenses for several months while her new company gets going.

Janet feels so strongly about her new direction that she's willing to give up a lot to get there. Her financial plan calls for almost no spending for entertainment. She traded in her car for a less expensive model. She stopped eating out and buying clothes. Her plan calls for as much money as possible to go towards debt reduction and building savings.

While not being able to spend for vacations and other treats is unpleasant at times, Janet's financial plan is making her happy. She is seeing rapid progress toward her dream of starting her own business.

Michael, on the other hand, is very comfortable in his life. He has recently received a promotion and has relatively low expenses. While Michael's plan does call for investing a significant amount, he also enjoys life. A Janet-style budget wouldn't fit his plans.

Without a burning need to drastically cut his expenses, his decision process is different from Janet's. He does budget money for personal items and entertainment, and he's planning for an upcoming vacation. He sees the plan as a way to keep him on track over the long term. And could follow it indefinitely.

Keeping your definition of success in mind as you formulate your plan will determine some of the choices you will make. You know where you want to go. You've even put a price on it. You also know where you are. Your financial plan combines these pieces of information.

Getting Started With A Plan

Start by looking at your financial snapshot. As you look at your one-page summary and the underlying data, work through questions like these:

- Does my income exceed my expenses? If the answer here is "no", use the strategies outlined in prior chapters to start to change your mindset. Until income is larger than expenses, it will be impossible to make financial progress.

- What is the price of my perfect life? You have thought about where you want to go and some of the costs of getting there.

- How soon do I want to be living my perfect life? Your choices in your financial plan will partly determine how quickly you reach your goals.

There are as many ways to develop a financial plan as there are financial planners. Some plans involve very complex analysis; others simple rules of thumb. You can find dozens of guidelines on the Internet or in the bookstore. Most of them have some good thoughts and can help you if you are totally stumped. But relying on someone else's plan (even mine) can only work if it's 100% in alignment with your own beliefs and goals.

Since we each come to the planning process from different perspectives, you will probably need to adjust the budget and other plan elements to suit your own priorities and goals. The bottom line is this: the only workable plan is one that is made just for YOU. If you see problem areas within this plan, you may need to adjust it to fit your own personal situation. If you think through the consequences of your changes, you can still develop a workable plan.

Key Elements Of A Successful Plan

While every plan is different, there are certain key elements that are common to a successful plan. As you develop your plan, consider and incorporate the following characteristics:

- *Fit Your Plan To Your Age:* Over the course of our lives, our financial situations change. Typically, income rises through the working years then drops upon retirement (for those employed in traditional work settings.) Expenses also grow as houses are purchased and children are born and so on, then may drop back again as debts are paid. This is also important as you consider various investment alternatives; what may be appropriate for a 25-year old may not be a good idea for a person nearing retirement.

- *Pay Yourself First:* Many of us make the mistake of saving money only if there's something left over at the end of the month. I can't emphasize enough how this can sabotage your efforts to reach your perfect life. For most people, the tendency is to spend whatever is available. In fact, most people (an estimated 7 out of 10) live *"paycheck to paycheck,"* meaning that all money coming in is immediately spent. By not investing in your own future and dreams FIRST, you are shortchanging yourself. My *caveat* here is if you are in debt. Pay yourself first by paying down your debts. You'll reduce your stress levels and begin to see clearer. Another way to pay yourself first is to pay yourself in time… the time to educate yourself.

- *Plan For Known, But Irregular, Expenses:* There are some expenditures that are not monthly but are predictable. Examples of these include holidays, car registration, annual insurance or tax payments, tuition, etc. It's far better to take charge of these and save for them in advance. For example, by setting money aside through the year to pay for a planned vacation, you can level off your spending needs, avoid expenses such as credit card finance charges after the fact, and avoid the stress of having to come up with the extra money all at once.

- *Plan For Unexpected Money Events:* All workable plans will deal with those expenses that will come up that you can't anticipate precisely. You may not be able to foresee what those are, but it is almost certain that there will be a need for extra cash now and then. If your plan doesn't lead to the creation of a cash reserve, the first unexpected money event (new tyres for the car, a broken computer, a medical bill, etc.) may leave you with few options.

- *Match The Budget To Your Income Level:* At various levels of income, the proportion of your spending that goes into some categories will change. For example, lower income budgets typically have a larger percentage flowing to categories such as housing and food, which are necessities.

The Basics Of Budgeting

Using your analysis of *"What Goes Out"* from your financial snapshot, you can calculate the percentage of your spending that falls into each major category. If it varied significantly over the time you tracked it, choose a *"middle-of-the-road"* estimate.

However, don't underestimate your expenses; be very honest with yourself. Once you have a realistic picture of your current allocation, you can pinpoint areas you want to reduce or expand.

One important decision about your budget is whether you're going to think in terms of *"gross"* income or *"net"* income. Gross income is your total salary for the time. Net income removes taxes and related amounts. It's often simpler to start with the net amount that you take home. Otherwise, you'll need to budget enough to cover all the taxes you will owe.

Starting from your net income and with some budget guidelines, you can calculate the amounts you *"should"* be spending in each category. Budget guidelines are available from various sources, one I find helpful for mid-range income levels is the following:

Budget Category	Target Percentage (of net income)
Savings	10%
Housing	30-35%
Car/transportation	10-15%
Loan Payments/Debt	5-10%
Insurance/Medical	5-10%
Utilities	5-10%
Food/eating out	10%
Clothing and personal items	5-15%
Entertainment/Recreation	10%

If your income is very high or very low, these percentages may need adjustment. Also, depending on where you live, housing may be more or less expensive. You may also have some categories that are difficult to control (such as medical) and find you need to cut back in other areas (such as recreation.)

Compare the percentages in the table above to those you calculated based on your own past spending patterns from your financial snapshot. Are you close? If not, where are the big differences? Are they good differences (such as you're saving more) or potential problems (such as you're spending far more for your car or entertainment)?

Notice that I put savings at the top of the list. Remember: pay yourself first! The 10% figure is a minimum, in my opinion. The more you can save and then invest, the faster you move along the path toward your perfect life. Work to make this component of your budget as high as you can—not as a goal, but to get to where you want to go with your finances. Spending for other things simply can't give you the freedom, flexibility and peace of mind that savings can bring. Think of it as an investment in your future.

The exception is if you currently have outstanding credit card or other high-interest debts you need to pay off. Because, once your debts have been paid off, you can redirect those payments into your savings account. You are already used to not having this money, so it will be easy to continue to save.

If your housing number is significantly higher, it can lead to problems throughout the process. Since housing is typically the largest expenditure category, if it's too high, the entire budget can get skewed. In addition, if your housing is expensive, it may also be more expensive to maintain, leading to higher figures for utilities, for example.

And in some parts of the country (such as urban areas) it can be difficult to locate housing that's more affordable. So, if you live in such an area, you may find that you must reduce your spending in other categories to compensate. You might consider reducing your housing cost by actions such as

- Selling and moving to a less-expensive house,

- Selling and renting for a while,

- Getting a housemate, or

- Checking on refinancing your house to see if you can lower your interest rate and, hence, your payment.

Another category which is a problem for many people, is their car. This is particularly true for those in lower-income groups. Even a relatively inexpensive car costs a lot to buy, drive, insure, and maintain. If you're spending is too high in this area, consider trading your car for one that is less expensive, at least until your income rises.

Loan payments and other debt is an area many people struggle to control. For some types of loans, it may be desirable to consolidate and lock in relatively low interest rates, thus saving on the total interest you pay. For other types, such as credit cards, interest charges quickly add up if you only make the minimum payment. Taking care of such loans is a priority.

The personal / clothing category is also a problem for many people. Spending for haircuts, designer clothes, cosmetics, facials / massages and other personal items can get way out of line.

However, most spending in this area is based on CHOICE rather than NECESSITY. You can take control of this area and reduce it.

You can stop your expensive habits by first examining the underlying reasons why you spend. Then, once you've found them, you can begin to deal with the real issues.

Any category that's way off the general guidelines can slow your progress (unless, of course, it's savings.) You may be willing to trade off one type of spending for another - live in a smaller house so you can drive a nicer car. Such exchanges are perfectly fine. After all, it's your money.

However, think carefully before you let categories such as personal / clothing or recreation get too far out of line. Such spending often brings pleasure for a very, very limited amount of time, and can jeopardize your efforts to take control of your money situation.

Planning When Your Income Varies

Many people are in situations where their income varies. Rather than a known amount coming in on a set day each week or each month, they may have somewhat unpredictable or variable income.

Salespeople who work on commission, for example, may receive pay when they make sales. And if you own a business, your ability to pull out a salary may be dependent on the profitability of the business.

Some people have income that's cyclical. Whatever your current situation, though, planning is still possible and desirable.

And if you have a variable income, you may need to consider some strategies such as:

- Planning over a longer period to account for variations through the year.

- Setting aside enough to cover living expenses so you can take care of your bills even during a "slow" income time.

- Saving even more in good times to offset your needs when your income isn't as high.

- Keeping a full month's expenses at the ready and replenishing as you do get paid.

- Taking on any increase in expenses only after very careful consideration of how you will pay for it during slower times.

- Using debt even more sparingly than you might otherwise to avoid locking in a large set of payments that might leave you with a cash flow problem during a low-income period.

Implementing Your Plan

Once you have a budget in place, you can begin to implement your plan. You may need a few months to get into alignment. Particularly if you need to make some major changes, such as your house or your car. As you take care of those things, also work to limit your spending in other areas to stay within your budget.

Begin to think about the little things you can do to reduce your unnecessary spending. When you get in the habit of being aware of how your money is getting away from you, you may find it helpful to make small changes. Changes that can yield real savings over time.

- You can turn down the heat in the winter and put on a sweater

- Take a free walk around the nearby park rather than paying for an expensive gym membership

- Do you really watch all the premium cable channels you have? Consider switching to basic cable or some other less-expensive option

- Brew your own coffee at home and take some with you to the office rather than stopping at the gourmet coffee shop

- Reduce the number of meals you eat out and learn to cook a few healthy and tasty dishes at home. Also, stay away from expensive processed and prepared foods when you visit the grocery store

- Go to the library and check out books rather than buying them

- Review your mobile phone, landline phone, and other utilities regularly to ensure your plans are still the best deal for you.

- Stop smoking

- Drink less alcohol

Believe it or not, you may find when you start to make these changes, your life improves in ways you never anticipated. When eating out becomes a treat rather than a habit, you're likely to enjoy it more. If you're a smoker and you quit the habit, your health will benefit. As well as your bank account.

There are entire websites and books about how to live less expensively. Some of the suggestions offered in such places require strong commitments, a lot of time, or a willingness to change your life in large ways. Others, however, are simple ideas that can build up into a real difference.

So, once you have your budget in place and are working to do even better, where should you start? Here are some steps and priorities:

The First Action To Take Is To Reduce Expensive, High-Interest Debt

There is nothing wrong with debt as a tool if it is used wisely. But expensive credit-card debt can be very bad for your long-term financial picture. While I have said (and I believe) that you must invest in yourself first by making savings a top priority; this doesn't apply if you have outstanding credit-card debts.

First, you need to stop using your cards. Cut them up if you must, but stop using them. Then pay them down and / or change them to a cheaper interest rate if possible.

By looking at the outstanding amounts and the 10% savings from your budget, you can begin to see how long it will take you to eliminate this debt. (Remember, though, interest charges will keep adding to the total even if you don't spend another dime.)

If you have balances on several cards and the interest rates vary, it makes sense to pay the minimums on all but the one with the highest rate. Pay down the highest rate card, then move to the next-highest rate and so on until they're all paid off.

Imagine the reduction in your stress levels when you pay off your last card. So, keep that in mind every time you're tempted to make another purchase.

Consider taking on an additional part-time job to bump up your income and allow you to pay these off faster. By avoiding future interest payments, you'll be doing yourself a big favor. The possibilities for additional streams of income have been previously discussed And paying off outstanding debts is a primary reason to consider some additional sources of income. Even if you couldn't maintain a second job forever, even a few months might allow you to make a significant dent in your outstanding bills.

If you're having big problems with credit card debt, consider talking to your creditors. Explain why you're having the difficulty and negotiate repayments on a schedule that gives you a little more breathing room. There are numerous credit counseling services available. They can provide wonderful advice and real help, but you should always ensure the agency you're dealing with is reputable.

Credit cards are a great financial tool, but the downside is they're so easy to use. And before you know it, you can run up balances that are more than you can afford. Setting up a nasty cycle of increasing interest payments and growing balances.

A good procedure is to write down every charge so that you always know how much you have outstanding on your cards, and then never go over the total you can pay in full when the statement comes.

Building A Cash Reserve Is Another Top Priority

As noted, you'll almost certainly be faced with unforeseen expenses. It is far better to plan for them and have some money set aside so that you aren't left with undesirable options such as having to run up big balances on credit cards. This is not the money you use for a choice, but the money you put aside for emergencies. Most experts recommend you set aside between two and six months of your living expenses in some sort of fund you can get your hands on if you lose your job or experience some other major financial problem. To start, aim for a smaller sum (such as $1000), which will cover most of what you'll likely face. If you must spend the reserve, replenish it as soon as possible. Consider it a loan to yourself. The peace of mind you can get from having a little money in the bank can be enormous.

Retirement Savings Are Essential

Far too many people put this off for too long. Many companies offer to match some part of your retirement savings. You should certainly look at taking advantage of this free money if you have access to such a plan.

Moreover, if you start young, your money can work for you, growing and earning interest over decades of time. For example, if you start saving a particular amount per year when you are in your mid-20s, you'll retire with twice as much as you'll have if you start just 10 years later.

Regular Bills Are Your Next Item To Consider

Don't discount the possibility of making real changes here. Do you own more house than you can comfortably afford? While the security of a home is important, a house that's too big and too expensive can erode your sense of security if you have to worry about how you'll afford it.

The recent mortgage credit crisis spotlighted the problems of some adjustable rate mortgages, with some people finding their housing costs suddenly skyrocketing as interest rate hikes took effect.

If you can only afford your house through some non-traditional financing such as a very low-down payment or a large amount due a few years out, you should consider whether you should make a change to reduce these kinds of risks.

In addition to the possibility of less-expensive housing, you may also be able to cut spending from other regular bills. Your car is an obvious category. Don't make the mistake of underestimating how much it costs to drive your car. In addition to the monthly payments, there are also expenses for petrol, maintenance, tyres, insurance, and registration.

Many people have eliminated their landline phones and are strictly using a mobile phone. Could this work for you? Would it reduce your expenses?

Look closely at your regular bills on a periodic basis. Don't pay more than is necessary just because you aren't paying attention. In some parts of Australia, for example, the retail market for electricity is open to competition. Is your electricity company giving you the most competitive rates?

Spending for personal items, clothing, recreation, travel, and so on can be a difficult category to control. While much of this is based on WANTS rather than NEEDS, it can still be hard to resist the temptations you're faced with in every storefront, website, magazine, newspaper, television, or radio ad. Once again, though, it's crucial you look to the real and lasting enjoyment you receive from these items.

Certainly, there are purchases which are well worth the money to you. If you can afford to, buying something you really want can be wonderful. However, if you overdo it, you can be left feeling out of control, watching as your debts pile up.

There are tricks and techniques to take control of your spending. I heard about a woman who didn't cut up her credit cards, but she did fill a bowl with water, drop in her cards, and put the entire thing in her freezer.

Her problem was, she tended to use the credit card for impulse purchases such as items advertised on television or something in a catalog that arrived in her mailbox.

Many times, she would discover that before the ice melted (and she could retrieve her cards), the urge to spend had passed. And she was relieved not to have spent her hard-earned cash. However, if she really did have a need, the cards were there.

Another trick I've heard, is to convert the budgeted amount for personal items into cash each month (or week or whatever time period you're using on your budget.) Once the cash is gone, the spending must stop. You may find this simple method of controlling spending very powerful. It takes you beyond numbers in a bank balance or the swipe of a credit card and makes the entire process more real.

At any moment, you can see the exact amount you still have free to spend and enjoy spending it knowing you're not over budget. You can also immediately see the implications of a purchase you're considering and how much (if any) you'll have left. It's a technique that may help you get in the habit of watching what you spend by increasing your awareness.

What To Do With A Windfall

Most of us have at some point been presented with a windfall. A lump sum of cash that comes to us, often unexpectedly. It may stem from an inheritance, a bonus from work, or even a lottery winning. Some people have a hard time deciding what to do with such a windfall. Many people end up spending it on trivial purchases that bring no lasting happiness.

In my opinion, the best use of a windfall is to move you faster in the direction you've already decided you want to go. Since you've already pictured your ideal life and thought about the best way to get there, why not use a windfall to speed you on your way?

If you have high-interest or credit card debt, a windfall is a great way to make a dent in or eliminate it. If you don't have such debt, use a cash infusion to set up an emergency fund in case of unexpected expenses.

It's not unreasonable to think about spending some portion of the windfall on something you really want to do or buy. After all, doing so doesn't affect your plan. However, don't waste the opportunity to take a giant step toward your perfect life.

Andrew and Jan had worked hard their entire adult lives. They'd never had very high incomes, but they had been able to stay out of debt for the most part. An unexpected bonus payment from work left them with a few thousand dollars.

And although they had no investments and little savings. Andrew and Jan decided to use the entire amount to go on a vacation they had been dreaming of for years. They went on the trip and had a pretty good time, although it didn't quite live up to their unrealistic expectations.

But within a few weeks', they were regretting their impulsive use of their money. Some unexpected medical bills left them with a large credit card debt to deal with and their stress began to rise. Yes, the vacation was nice. But Andrew and Jan never considered the cash might bring them more long-term benefits if used in a different way.

If you are fortunate enough to receive a windfall, follow the plan you've already made. Pay down credit card bills, set up a cash reserve, or save / invest it.

Consider the windfall as an opportunity to leap ahead toward the life you want to live. Spend some little piece, perhaps, but use most of it to move closer to your financial goals. Remember to sacrifice in the short term to reap the greater returns in the long term.

Contingency Plans

What if something really goes wrong? While it can be difficult to think about such things, it can also bring enormous peace of mind to know you have done what you can to plan ahead. This doesn't mean you live in fear.

It's important to consider what happens if your earning power disappears. If other people are financially dependent on you (your husband / wife, your children or others), it's crucial to have a contingency plan, just in case you're forced to stop work.

In addition to saving a few months' worth of living expenses, I recommend looking at both life insurance and disability insurance policies. If you're involved in an accident or suffer an illness, having the proceeds from these policies may be essential to you and / or your loved ones.

Life insurance can be surprisingly affordable, and most insurers offer free consultations. By insuring your financial security, even if something bad happens, you'll also buy yourself peace of mind.

A Final Note On Planning

As noted at the outset, a good financial plan can be very liberating. Although it may certainly involve some discipline, it's also an important component in achieving real and sustainable wealth.

The budgets mentioned previously are simply guidelines to get you started. They can help you take control of your current situation and start to change it to move you in the right direction. However, they're only the first step.

Once you can stick to a budget, you'll see your income start to outweigh your expenses. With a little time, you'll see your debts start to shrink while your savings grow. At that point, you're ready to start your investment program in earnest. The more your income exceeds your expenses, the faster you can move forward towards your financial goals.

In the next chapter, we'll talk about some of the variety of investment options. These are ways you can put your money to work for YOU. A well-crafted investment strategy can bring you financial security and wealth.

The key is to come up with a budget that works for you. Factor in your goals and the specifics of your situation. Keep in mind your ultimate destination: your perfect life. Before you know it, you'll be moving in the right direction.

For Further Thought:

Making A Plan To Change Your Financial Image

1. In this chapter, you worked to compile a specific financial plan and budget. When you compare your past spending to your future budget spending, where are the biggest changes going to occur?

    _____

    _____

    _____

    _____

    _____

    _____

2. When you look at these changes, which do you think will be the most difficult for you?

    _____

    _____

    _____

    _____

    _____

    _____

3. Remember, this plan provides a roadmap to your perfect life. I encourage you to think about and write down a short statement of affirmation of your desire to take control of your finances through your plan. Here's an example; adapt it as you wish.

I can and will take control of my spending.

I have the power to shape my financial image.

I choose to change the way I use money so that I can reach my goals and achieve my dreams.

_____

_____

_____

_____

_____

_____

_____

_____

*If you don't want to write in your book… You can download all the exercises at:
www.TheMoneyMirrorBook.com/resources

Rae Brent

Chapter 9

Discovering The Best Way To Get To Where You Want To Go

T he sooner you begin to invest your money, the faster you'll begin to move toward the life you want. Once you put your money to work through a solid investment plan, it begins to work for you through earning interest or dividends, increasing in value, or yielding profits.

Through the prior chapters, you have identified how you want to look in your *Money Mirror*. You've also probably begun to rethink the way you spend and save. I hope you're taking control of your finances. Once you've paid off your high-interest debt and set aside a cash reserve, it's time to invest.

Investing can be intimidating and overwhelming at first. There is so much information (and misinformation) out there, that it can be difficult to separate the good ideas from the rest.

This is also complicated by facts such as the following:

- Financial news surrounds us from the television, radio, Internet, newspapers, and magazines.

- Most people have an opinion about the best way to invest money and many are quick to tell you about it. This is particularly true of family and friends.

- Our limiting beliefs and other components of our personalities can come into play and make decisions more difficult.

- Some people offering investments have a vested interest in influencing you to make choices that are best for THEM, not always for YOU.

- By their very nature, investments are unpredictable. There are no guarantees they'll perform the way they did in the past. Or even that they'll not drop in value.

Even with these issues (and the list could go on and on), it's still crucial to develop an investment strategy that works for you. If you have never invested money before, it can be somewhat frightening to give up control of your hard-earned savings. If you've had a bad investing experience, it can be even harder.

However, it's virtually impossible to build sustainable wealth if your money never works for you. Even if you kept all your savings in a box under your bed, you'd slowly, but surely, see its value shrink as inflation eroded its purchasing power.

There's an incredible array of investment options available. Some are quite risky. While others are relatively safe. By keeping in mind, the path, you want to travel, to get to your chosen financial situation. You'll easily be able to identify investments to fit in with your goals.

Many tools are available to help you in this decision process. Some of the best I've seen are available free from sources such as the Securities and Exchange Commission (SEC) in the US. Their website walks you step-by-step through the process.

Other good sites, complete with tools to help you calculate future needs, are maintained by several of the large financial publishers. I strongly encourage you to use these to help you understand the nature of investing.

A quick word of caution though. On any given day, the volume of information can be enough to make you begin to second guess prior choices or change your mind about your direction. It's crucial to remember you're looking toward a long-term goal. Don't be distracted from your purpose because of the latest opinions splashed across the headlines.

Also remember many of the people you see interviewed on television have an agenda. They are trying to make a specific point and may not be presenting a balanced view. Be careful of trying to incorporate every single viewpoint or idea into your investment strategy.

In the following sections, I want to describe a few of the big questions you'll need to answer in your own mind as you move forward in the investment process. This is, by design, a discussion to make you begin to get comfortable with your OWN capabilities to choose wisely from the thousands of options available.

There are hundreds of investment guides, strategies, and recommendations in bookstores and on websites. Financial planning professionals working in banks, securities firms, and other companies can offer great advice. The problem many people have is in CHOOSING a strategy that fits their own situation.

I chose real estate investing partly because it interests me, for example. However, this is not to say it's right for YOU. It takes a lot of time to keep up with the latest trends in the market place. And my properties, my tenants, and all the rest that's involved with such a strategy. I enjoy it though, and it doesn't feel like work to me. You may find you're interested in something similar, but you may not. Over the years, I've identified what works for me, and you will, too.

The remainder of this chapter presents some basic concepts you need to consider before you invest. Think about these areas and use them as you sift through the potential directions for your investment strategy.

Note, this is NOT investment advice. I cannot and would not presume to know enough about you and your financial situation to make specific recommendations. Instead, it's more a way of thinking about how to choose your own investment strategy. One that'll fit you best and help you achieve your own goals.

Financial advisors or investment guides can help you work up the specifics of your own plan, but before you invest a single dollar or talk to a professional advisor, there are several things you need to consider.

How Soon Will You Need Your Money?

Picking the right way to save or invest your money depends in part on how soon you'll need it. Some investments are easy (and inexpensive) to buy and sell. Others are more involved. Some also vary in value over time more than others.

Many types of savings accounts and investment vehicles offer well-defined returns. For any funds you'll need in a short period of time, these may be the best options.

Your age is relevant, because it helps you determine how soon you'll need your money. If you're approaching retirement and will need to start pulling money out of your investments. You won't want to sink your cash into anything that's hard to get out of when you need it.

On the other hand. If you're in your 20s and are looking for a good place to invest for a very long time, you'll have different options.

Consider the timing of when you'll need your money back. Are there large expenses coming up right away that you'll need your investments to pay for? Do you plan to buy a house or make some other major purchase at some point? When? Are you close to retiring and will need your money?

Risk And Return

One of the most important considerations as you begin to invest is risk and return. Investments fall somewhere along a spectrum from *"very safe"* to *"very risky."*

A very safe investment is one that's extremely unlikely to decrease in value. For example, one of the safest investments in the world is US Treasury bonds and bills. The US government backs these investments and defines the interest they will yield. Savings accounts insured by the government are also safe. However, these *"safe"* investments pay relatively low rates of return.

At the other end of the spectrum are very risky investments. These are the kind that may pay off big... IF they pay off at all!

You may also earn nothing. And you could lose your entire investment.

In general, lower risk yields lower returns and higher risk yields higher returns. However, there are some *"investments"* that are so uncertain they aren't worth the risk. You may know someone or have heard stories of people who made a great deal of money in some very risky investments. It happens.

However, there are also those who invested and lost. If a scheme sounds *"too good to be true,"* you need to trust your intuition and investigate very thoroughly before you decide to commit or not.

Think about the level of risk you are willing to tolerate. Remember that putting all your money in a savings account may be the safest, but it also won't earn you much (if anything, when you consider inflation.)

One strategy is to divide your investments among several options of varying risk. You might put the bulk of your money (at least until you have a comfortable nest egg) into moderate-risk strategies that will give you decent returns. With some percentage of your investment money, you might go into somewhat riskier options.

But never invest more than you can afford or are willing to lose.

Your risk tolerance is driven in part by your personality. Some people are comfortable with a little more risk if the returns justify it. Others lose sleep over the fact the values of their investments fluctuate. Which are you? As a preliminary step in the process of formulating your investment strategy, it's a good idea to think through your own comfort level with risk.

The question of how soon you'll need your money also plays a role in the level of risk you choose to accept. The value of some types of investments can change quickly. And while this is less of a problem if you are investing for a long time. And you can choose when you want to sell. It can be a problem if you need the money suddenly. You may be forced to take a loss on an investment if you must sell during a period when its value is down.

Risk tolerance is a very personal decision. It's also an area where you can sometimes be irrational. Again, if you put your money in a very safe investment that earns very little return, you have ensured you won't lose it outright.

However, without enough of a return, what that money can buy you will decrease over time. You'll also make little or no progress toward building your wealth.

A thorough understanding of risk is, therefore, essential to effective investing. In the investment world, some risk IS worth taking.

Diversification

There is an old saying that you shouldn't *"put all of your eggs in one basket."* The idea of course is, if something happens to your single basket, you could lose everything.

If you invest in a single stock or share, your entire return depends on that one company. So, for example, if you bought shares in a huge oil company and the price of oil dropped drastically. You'd lose your money, if that was the only stock you'd invested in. Even though many other stocks and shares may increase in value due to the drop-in oil prices.

The idea of diversification is that you invest in different industries in the hope that as one goes down, others will go up.

You are, in theory, more protected from the types of events that affect specific companies.

In the example above, if you had shares in the oil company AND shares in an airline. You might see the oil company shares decrease in value, but you may come out okay because your airline shares increased in value. Thanks to the lower fuel prices the airline would have to pay because oil was now less expensive.

There are many books available that can teach you, in more detail, how you can best diversify your investments. An easy way to diversify within the stock market, however, is by purchasing mutual funds instead of shares in individual companies.

Mutual funds purchase shares in a variety of companies. You can, in turn, buy some of the mutual fund's shares and in effect hold portions of each stock. There are hundreds of mutual fund-type investment options available. They also involve varying levels of risk.

Companies that sell shares in such funds generate detailed statements of the fund's holdings and other detailed information including the fund managers' objectives. Before you invest in anything, you should carefully do your Due Diligence.

You can also diversify by investing in totally different types of investment vehicles. I have found that the best option for me is to place some of my money in shares and other securities and some in real estate and some in business. This is another level of diversification in that even if the entire market for shares and stocks is dropping, the real estate market and business sector may be growing.

Another aspect of diversification is to consider what you already have invested. This would include your house (you may already be in real estate.) You should also consider your job (particularly if your employer grants you shares or options for shares as part of your compensation.)

If you work in an industry, it can be a wise strategy to be sure you aren't getting too financially dependent on that one industry.

In the example above, if you work for a huge oil company and oil prices go down, you might lose your job. Therefore, you wouldn't want to be overly invested in oil stocks, which would also be going down.

Again, a full discussion of the specifics of diversification is beyond the scope of this book. My goal is to make you think about the issue and how you can protect yourself by ensuring you don't invest too much of your hard-earned income in a single direction.

How To Evaluate Potential Investments

It's time to get started when you have thought through questions such as these:

- How much do you have to invest and when will you need it back?

- How much risk are you comfortable with, given your personality?

- Where are you currently invested and how might you diversify?

Even if you hire someone to help you. You need to have some confidence in your own ability to evaluate the potential for the investment. And how it fits into your path to your financial goals.

It's also a great idea to increase your financial vocabulary. I've found Robert Kiyosaki's book, *"Rich Dad, Poor Dad"* a great place to start.

One of the first criteria is to be sure the investment is legitimate. There are very persuasive scam artists looking to take away your savings through *"get-rich-quick"* schemes. Many of which have very little merit.

I saw this happen all too often with friends who left military service with a substantial sum of money. Money that could have been the foundation for sustainable wealth. Rather than putting the money into an investment program that would yield real results, they were taken in by promises of very rapid and very high returns.

Again, if an investment seems *"too good to be true,"* there's a very good chance it is. Analyze the fine print and investigate thoroughly rather than purchasing the first shiny and promising thing you see.

Be sure you thoroughly understand what you're purchasing. Investigate whether the company or individual involved is registered with the securities agencies. Check for complaints. Search the Internet for evidence of investigations into the individuals or companies involved. See if you can find support for the legitimacy of the opportunity.

If anything raises concerns, don't commit until you are fully reassured and presented with evidence that you're not being *"taken for a ride."* If you don't understand what you're buying, you might be better off to keep looking. Far too many people have lost thousands. Don't be too hasty to jump into the first opportunity you see. It's better to miss out on a good deal (there's always another if you keep looking), than to lose your money in a scam.

Next, determine whether the investment fits your goals. Is it too risky? Are the returns too low? Would it require you to wait too long before you could sell? Does it represent good diversification for you? Would it require too much of your time to manage? If the investment fails on any of these criteria, move on.

You need to know exactly how much you'll be investing. How much it will cost (through commissions, for example), and what fees (if any) are involved. Ask how much you would get back if you sold your position immediately. This will tell you the amount of up-front fees and other hidden costs.

Know how easy or difficult it would be to sell. Many securities investments can be sold with a simple phone call or click of a mouse. Partial ownership of a business can be very difficult (if not impossible) to sell. Would it be costly to sell?

Be sure you know about all the risks of the investment. Is it vulnerable if the economy slows? Is it dependent on one industry? Is there a key individual involved and would it be negatively affected if that individual backed out? Are there other issues which can change the potential return, such as a patent (or lack thereof)? What about any outstanding lawsuits or complaints?

If you're buying a security, ask how it's performed in the past. Compare its performance to other securities with similar risks. Get copies of the related documents such as the latest prospectus and other filings with regulatory agencies.

This list is certainly not designed to be exhaustive, and there are many other potential problems or issues that could arise with any investment. Thoroughly investigate before you commit. Use your intuition, and if it sounds too good to be true, be particularly cautious. Understand that anyone selling an investment has an interest in convincing you to buy. Look at it from all angles. Compare it to your financial goals. If it appears to be a good fit, look to uncover any potential downside. If you can't get enough evidence to convince you that it's legitimate, stay away.

There are plenty of investment options which are very easy to investigate. Shares and funds, for example, are relatively easy to understand. While there's no guarantee of their performance and their value could certainly fall, they are easier to investigate due to the stringent requirements of the regulatory agencies.

After thoroughly researching, you should be able to tell if an opportunity is a good fit for your investment criteria regarding timing, risk, costs, and other factors. Such analysis will help you determine if it's a place you'd like to put your money to work.

How To Find Additional Help

With all the complexities in investing, it can be a wonderful idea to bring in an investment professional to help. Such a person should be keeping up with the markets for shares, bonds, and other options. They should be familiar with tax implications and have a feel for how markets are changing. Given that investments are their occupation, they should also be better able to keep up with the massive amounts of information which determine values and risk. In addition, some types of investment strategies can be very complicated and difficult to implement.

Hiring a professional in no way means you have to give up control. It's still YOUR money. In fact, it's a bad idea to assume any investment professional will always make the right choice for you 100% of the time. They are there to help, but you're the only one who can make the ultimate decision.

Unfortunately, there are many unscrupulous investment professionals out there. Some of these people are incompetent, dishonest, or otherwise undesirable as a part of your investment team. Many others, however, are highly intelligent and enormously informed and can help you put together the best plan to achieve your goals.

Financial advisors may make their money from the commissions they receive when they buy shares or funds for you. Or they may charge a set fee for their services. Their help may be free of charge to you if they're working on commission. Some banks offer investment planning as a part of their service to customers. You may be able to get great advice without it costing you anything. The argument in favor of set fees is, it removes the temptation for the financial advisor to steer you into investments based on prospective commissions.

So how do you protect yourself from bad advisors? With research! You must thoroughly investigate any professional you plan to use. Does the person or their firm have a history of complaints with regulatory agencies? In the US, people or firms who are paid to give advice about investing in securities generally must be registered and maintain a registration form called the "Form ADV," which includes information about whether they've had problems with clients or regulators, how their fees work, their strategies, and so on.

All countries with well-developed securities markets have accompanying well-developed regulation of those markets. Wherever you live, you can find the regulatory agencies at work registering and monitoring investment professional and advisory firms. You can typically receive information on any complaints or problems simply by asking.

You should also ask questions about the professional's training and experience. You can ask about numbers of clients and characteristics of typical clients. It's crucial to understand how the advisor is paid and what it will cost you to utilize their services. They should also be able to tell you about their own investment philosophy.

Also ask them about their own investment strategies. This may just be a job for them and they may have no real investing experience. Find someone who is *"walking their talk"* in investing before following their advice.

Any of these areas can lead you to realize a person is not a good fit. If you don't believe they have adequate training or knowledge, for example, you should look elsewhere. If they are paid on commission, you should be aware that they may have an incentive to suggest types of investments. If you are uncomfortable with their understanding of you as a potential client or if you disagree with their investment philosophy, you should keep searching.

If you do decide to get additional help, your advisor should ask you about your investment goals and financial situation, risk tolerance, and time horizon for investing. Since you have developed a thorough understanding of these from your work through this book, you can provide answers to such questions. You can also examine any suggestions considering your own decisions regarding your path to wealth.

An investment advisor can be a tremendous help in working up a detailed plan for reaching your financial goals. Because you have considered these issues yourself, you are better able to judge the validity of the professional's advice as well as whether it fits your chosen path.

Getting To Know Your Three (3) V's

One concept that has made the world of difference in my own personal wealth creation and that of my clients has been the ability to align each potential wealth creation strategy / opportunity with their 3V's.

The 3V's are:

- Vision
- Values
- Vibration

All too often you may allow *"shinny objects"* to grab your attention (i.e. going after the next *"get rich quick scheme."*) You can see, on the surface, just how great an opportunity it's made out to be by the person selling it. But unless it's in alignment with your 3V's, it usually becomes something in your life that you regret over time.

A huge energetic disparity is created when what you are doing is out of alignment with your Values, Vision and Vibration. You may be left feeling low, depressed or overwhelmed. And, by keeping in alignment with your 3V's, you can live the life you truly deserve. But you need to know what they are first.

What are your…Values, Vision and Vibration? Take some time to have a closer look at yourself and your life.

So, the next time an opportunity doesn't quite feel right, check to see if it fits in with your 3V's. Because, when you're in full alignment with them, you will be in your flow. And that's when you'll start to generate great sustainable wealth in all aspects of your life.

Getting Started

Once you understand your inner strengths, goals, desires and your 3V's. You can better match them to one of the many investment programs which are readily available. You can choose with more confidence, because you've thought through what you're trying to accomplish.

Remember the vehicle analogy? Recall how it's impossible to decide what kind of vehicle is best for you if you don't know where you want to go. You need to know what the roads will be like, and what the vehicle will need to carry. It's the same for investments. You can't possibly recognize a good opportunity if you don't have an idea of your goals and priorities.

Now that you've thought through you own idea of financial success and the way you think you want to go to get there, you can identify the investment vehicles that are right for you. You can begin to look at the thousands of opportunities in a new way. Discard the ones that may be great for other people, but don't work for you.

Over the years, I've collected pieces of investment advice by reading hundreds of books from many authors and attending countless numbers of seminars. I've combined those pieces of information into an investment strategy that works for me. It shapes how I earn my money and how I invest it.

You'll find the more you learn, the deeper your understanding will become. You'll start to pick out your own pieces of information - the ones that really work for you. And they'll help you to attain your perfect life.

I believe Buddha said it best when he said…

Believe nothing... No matter where you read it, or who said it... Not even if I have said it... Unless it agrees with your own reason, and your common sense

Don't become overwhelmed by the jargon and complexity of investing. Yes, there's a lot to know if you want to understand all the potential investment types. However, such a level of knowledge isn't necessary to develop the beginnings of a sound investment strategy.

Investigate one of the programs from a reputable source and see if it fits your goals. Do your research to see if it fits into what you want to achieve. If not, check out another investment vehicle.

When you decide on an investment vehicle, learn and understand as much about it as you can. The more you learn about and apply yourself to driving your investment vehicle, the quicker you'll achieve your perfect life.

Whatever you do, just get started. Remember the sooner you begin investing, the sooner your money will start working for you.

For Further Thought:

Discovering The Best Way To Get To Where You Want To Go

1. As you get ready to begin your investment program, you'll need to make some decisions about the types of assets you'll invest in. Will they be shares, bonds, or other marketable securities or do you find more *"hands-on"* type investments (such as real estate or a small business) more appealing? What if any types of investments have you heard about in the past that seemed interesting to you?

    _____

    _____

    _____

    _____

    _____

    Which of these do you think are worth investigating further?

    _____

    _____

    _____

    _____

2. An important consideration in your investment strategy is when you will need your money. Think about upcoming needs for significant funds for major purchases (such as a house or car), retirement, and so on. What needs do you see

for getting your money back out of your investments coming in the next 2 years?

_____

_____

_____

_____

What about the next 5 years?

_____

_____

_____

_____

The next 10 years?

_____

_____

_____

_____

3. When you think about investment risk, what emotions come into play? Do you feel sick thinking about changes in share values causing the value of your investments to rise and fall? Do you see such short-term changes as a normal part of investing and thus feel comfortable with the inevitable shift in values? What would stop you from sleeping at night regarding investing?

_____

_____

_____

_____

_____

4. Where are you currently investing? Look at the things you own section of your financial snapshot. Where are your assets? In your house? Shares of stock in particular industries?

_____

_____

_____

_____

_____

_____

_____

5. How diversified is your investment portfolio right now? Do you see actions you need to take to add diversity?

_____

_____

_____

_____

_____

_____

_____

_____

*If you don't want to write in your book… You can download all the exercises at:
www.TheMoneyMirrorBook.com/resources

Chapter 10

Today Is The Day To Change

C ongratulations on reading this far. Give yourself a pat on the back.

So, to quickly recap… Throughout this book you've:

- Thought about what your life would be like if you didn't have to think about money,

- Considered your perceptions about your money situation and why you might not be thinking clearly about your finances,

- Analyzed your current financial situation,

- Developed an idea of how you want your finances to look and thought about how you want to get there,

- Evaluated your beliefs about yourself and how they might be keeping you from achieving your dreams,

- Created a financial plan including a budget to help you move in the directions you want to go,

- Formulated an understanding of how you feel about investments and investing so that you can begin to build wealth, and

- Thought about some of the pitfalls that might challenge you on your path to your perfect life.

My goal throughout this process was NOT to present a structured, one-size-fits-all magic answer for achieving sustainable wealth. And frankly, there's no such thing. Each of us brings past experiences, special talents / skills, goals and dreams to the process.

This isn't to say we can't learn by studying such plans. Many authors, speakers, and thinkers have offered wonderful perspectives on these issues. However, if you don't know where YOU want to go or what YOU believe, you'll have little chance of success with anyone else's process.

The best way to achieve sustainable wealth is to connect with your deepest-held beliefs, dreams, and strengths. Use existing plans and theories as tools, but place them within the context dictated by your inner self.

Remember back to the vehicle analogy. If you go into the dealership, they can tell you all about their cars. They know them inside and out (if they're good salespeople.) They'll mention every advantage their car can offer. You know from the outset they have an agenda - to sell you one of the cars on their lot - because that's how they make their money.

However, even a totally honest salesperson can't know what's best for you. Only you can decide. Once you know what you want and need, you can choose the appropriate dealership to go to. You can ask the right questions. And you can make the best decision for YOU.

It's the same with your money. All the investment advice, guidance, plans, and prescriptions won't do you any good if it isn't going to get you what YOU want. You also won't have much success sticking with a plan if you don't have a strong idea about why you're doing so.

The advice, tools, and thoughts of other people can certainly be helpful, but only if you have already thought about where you're going and what path is right for you. With that knowledge, it is possible to evaluate various options, plans, and investment strategies within the right framework. You can then pick the pieces that fit for you.

Visualize Your Perfect Life

Professional athletes from many sports have described the technique of visualization to enhance their performance. Prior to a game, match, round, or other contest, they imagine the perfect performance as part of their preparation.

For example, a golfer might picture him or herself on the number one tee box with driver in hand. In very vivid detail, they imagine the perfect swing. They see the ball flying through the sky to land hundreds of yards away in the middle of the fairway. And they imagine hitting the perfect iron shots and putts to sink the ball into the cup.

This positive visualization can have an enormous effect on your success. It's purposefully feeding your subconscious mind the right messages. And it has a calming and strengthening effect, as your body responds to the positive thoughts.

Visualizing your perfect life is one of the keys to achieving it. Every day, set aside some time to remind yourself where you want to go with your life. Recall the reasons you're in the process of changing your financial habits and patterns to make your dreams come true. Make this mental picture full of detail. Imagine what you see, what you hear, and how you feel. The more realistic this vision is, the more power it'll be for you.

Picture yourself resisting your financial temptations. Imagine how it feels the day your credit card debt is totally paid off. Think about the freedom you'll have when you can cut your work hours to part time because your money is working for you.

Whatever your dream or goal, you can visualize yourself achieving it. In this way, you'll keep yourself motivated to stay on track. You'll also feed your powerful subconscious mind the right messages. Even just a few minutes each day. Particularly when you're feeling tempted to overspend or otherwise slip from your chosen path. You can make a real difference. Not only to your mental state, but also to the time it takes to achieve your goals.

Celebrate Your Progress

I hope you've already begun to change your image in *The Money Mirror*. Even if you haven't made much progress YET. I want to assure you, you're moving in the right direction by making a plan.

It can help you stick with your long-term goals if you celebrate your progress. As you reach milestones along your path (such as paying off one of your credit cards or investing a certain amount), find an appropriate way to celebrate.

As a society, we tend to celebrate by spending money. But you can be different. My point is to mark your progress, not derail it. Celebrations can be very simple and inexpensive or even free. They can be important rewards and reminders you ARE moving towards your goals, dreams and your perfect life.

The Sooner... The Easier!

It can be tempting to put off taking control of your financial situation. You may keep going as you've been going, always thinking that you'll do it *"tomorrow."* While it may take some time to get your financial snapshot and plan together, it's time well spent. It's an investment in your future, and the longer you wait, the more difficult it'll become.

If your current money habits are causing you problems, such as spending more than your income. The longer you wait, the bigger the issue will be. Because, if you don't stop overspending now, your debt level will continue to grow.

Being late with payments can cause interest to spike even more than if your rates rise (a typical condition with many credit card companies.) You need to start NOW to stop digging yourself into an ever-deeper debt hole.

In addition, the sooner you start, the faster your money will begin to grow and work for you. As it grows, it earns more money. There's a classic example which illustrates this concept.

What if I offer to give you a cent today and twice that amount tomorrow? What if I offer to double the amount I give you each day. How much do you think the amount would be in a week? What about in two weeks? Or in a month?

The answer might surprise you. On the eighth day, I would give you $1.28, obviously not much. However, by day 15, the amount would be up to $163.84. And by the end of the month on day 31, I'd be handing you $10,737,418!!!!

While investments can't be expected to double every day, the implication is clear. When your money starts to grow (through interest paid to you, dividends, and increasing value of what you own), its power to generate even more returns also grows. You start earning interest on the interest you've been paid, and then you earn interest on that interest. This idea, known as compounding, is a crucial aspect of most paths to sustainable wealth.

The longer you wait, the less time you have for this compounding to work for you. Remember the example earlier in the book of the person who starts saving for retirement in their 20s compared to the person who begins in their 30s. By retirement age, the same amount of savings has grown twice as large for the 20-year old saver thanks to compounding.

Take control of your money and put it to work for you. Remember, the sooner, the better!

Start Small... And Start Now!

Have you heard the old saying that *"a journey of 1,000 miles begins with one step?"* Sometimes, it can seem overwhelming to compare where you are now to where you want to be. The debts you face may seem insurmountable. Fighting your belief systems may feel exhausting. Changing your habits may feel impossible.

Few people reach their goals overnight, though. When you consider where they are today, you also must remember where they came from. Because even the wealthiest and most influential people in our world today (such as Oprah Winfrey or Sir Richard Branson) faced enormous struggles as they worked to achieve their dreams.

These people were not afraid to keep their dreams alive through thick or thin. Even when they seemed to be making little, if any progress. They didn't start out the incredibly wealthy and successful people you see today. So, don't let yourself get trapped into believing there's no way you could reach so high.

Remember, there's no such thing as *"an overnight success."* And every Master was once a disaster!

One of my mentors, Dan Kennedy, says *"small hinges swing big doors!"* Small changes can have big payoffs. By taking one step toward your perfect life, it will be a step in the right direction. Don't put it off because it seems too big or too difficult.

Just a few dollars each day can make a difference. Think of a small amount at first—a number that'll be relatively easy to find out of your monthly budget. Drop a dollar into a bowl each time you go out your front door. Take out $10 each time you cash a check and put it aside. Over time, these small amounts will grow.

Look at your expenses. What small thing can you live without today? Can you spend a little time cooking dinner tonight and save yourself some money? Could you skip the movie at the cinema and rent a DVD instead or even read a book?

Radical changes can be upsetting, and we tend to avoid them if they have the potential to make us feel uncomfortable. If you can't imagine selling your too-expensive house, getting rid of your pricey car, and totally changing your spending habits overnight, I don't blame you. Make a plan to do these things over time if you need to do so.

Any changes for the better are better than none. Even if you don't see how you can possibly do it all right now, make a commitment to at least do something. Start small and start now. Once you get going, you may find those so called tough changes easier.

Remember to set yourself up for success, rather than failure.

Know What You Want And What's Keeping You From Getting There

A clear understanding of your reflection in *The Money Mirror* is essential to reaching your dreams. Knowing where you stand today is crucial. The next step is to know where you want to go.

You should now have a very clear picture of your perfect life. You know what it's like and you even have some idea of what it costs. You visualize it daily. It keeps you on track, motivated, and focused. Decisions are easier to make because you can see how they fit within your path to your goals.

It's also important to know what the obstacles are that you are facing. Are you filled with self-doubt or other limiting beliefs? Are you feeding your subconscious mind the wrong images? Without a clear and well-developed understanding of where you're going, it is very difficult to stick to a plan or choose the right investment vehicle.

Until you set yourself a goal, you won't encounter *"obstacles."*

Let Go Of Limiting Beliefs

I can't overemphasize how damaging self-limiting beliefs can be. They can cause you to pass up opportunities or stick with things that just aren't right for you. Sometimes, these limiting beliefs are the biggest blocks to reaching your goals.

Unfortunately, they're not likely to change without a conscious effort. So, unless you think specifically about them and work to let go of them, they will continue to affect you for your entire life.

And you DO have the power to let them go. The first step is to have conscious recognition of them. Because, when you know what they are, you can replace them with more empowering beliefs.

So, now that you've begun to identify your limiting beliefs, I encourage you to stay vigilant. When you find your limiting beliefs creeping into your thoughts, take control and change them. There's great freedom in letting go. So don't spend another day haunted by self-doubt or filled with the drive to acquire *"shiny objects"* that don't serve you.

Whatever the source of your limiting beliefs, YOU ALONE can let them go. There's no reason why you need to live in the drama.

You Have The Power To Change

You control your money. Your money doesn't control you. Sometimes, we forget this simple fact. Money is simply paper or numbers on a page or a balance on an account. It has no power of its own. It doesn't decide to spend itself, nor does it jump into investments without you.

YOU are the one with the power to change, and there's no reason to wait. Even if you've struggled before, chances are you were unclear about where you were going, and you didn't find the right path. Maybe you didn't see clearly where you were from the start. It can be hard at times to stick to your plan, but the rewards make it worthwhile.

Other people may be of great help to you, but the final responsibility for your life resides with you. Even loved ones don't have the power to change your beliefs about yourself (though they certainly can influence them one way or the other.)

No friend or neighbor or parent or spouse or son or daughter can offer you the magic answer to your financial issues.

However, with a clear vision of where you want to be and a determination to stick to your plan to get there, you can make a real change. You DO have the power.

Are You Ready?

No one lives forever. You have no guarantee of your health. Years pass by whether you like it or not. Children grow up and parents age.

Are you spending your life the way you want to? Or are you stuck in a job you dislike. Working for a boss you don't even respect? Are money worries or a sense things are out of control wearing you down?

Commit to making a real change for yourself and making it now. The sooner you get going, the faster you'll arrive. It's up to you. Look inside yourself and you will find the power to change.

It has been said within spiritual circles, that the most enlightened words ever spoken by a human, were spoken by Joseph Campbell when he said, *"Follow Your Bliss."*

Pauline Longdon has taken this one step further by saying *"Live Your Bliss"* instead of just following it!

This way, you own your life instead of constantly chasing something you'll never catch.

Pauline and I've combined this statement with Gandhi's quote *"Be the change you want to see in the world."* And we now have an amazing mantra to live our lives by, which is:

> *Be the change you want to see in*
> *the world ...by living your bliss!*
>
> – Gandhi, Joseph Campbell and Pauline Longdon

Your perfect life is waiting for you. Are you ready? You CAN have it all NOW! And you DESERVE to Have it all Now!!!

Go on, give yourself permission to have it all now.

What will you see when you look in YOUR *Money Mirror*?

Only You get to decide. So…

Decide – Commit – Act
...Your Time is NOW!

It's time to connect with your inner self and create *Great Sustainable Wealth* in all aspects of your life.

I want to congratulate you for reaching this point in the book. So, well done. Create your reality and *Live Your Bliss!*

I hope you'll make it a great one!

With Love, Light and Abundance… Rae

For Further Thought:

Today Is The Day To Change

1. What are some of the milestones along your path towards your financial goals?

    _____
    _____
    _____
    _____
    _____
    _____

2. How will you celebrate passing these milestones? What about when you achieve your goals?

    _____
    _____
    _____
    _____
    _____
    _____

3. What are the major challenges you face as you work to change your financial image (self-limiting beliefs, for example)?

    _____
    _____
    _____
    _____
    _____
    _____

4.   What small change can you make TODAY that'll move you closer to your goals?

_____

_____

_____

_____

_____

_____

_____

5.   If you had to summarize your perfect life and how you plan to get there, what would you say?

_____

_____

_____

_____

_____

_____

_____

6.   What do you feel is holding you back and how do you plan to change it?

_____

_____

_____

_____

_____

_____

_____

7.   If you had to write a statement of your commitment to taking control of your finances and starting down your path to your perfect life TODAY, what would it say? Here is an example, change it as you like.

Today is MY day. I AM now in control of money. I have the power to change my financial situation, and I WILL use that power to move toward my goals and my perfect life. I choose to let go of my self-doubt and negative feelings right now. My perfect life is waiting, and I AM READY!

_____

_____

_____

_____

_____

_____

_____

*If you don't want to write in your book... You can download all the exercises at:
www.TheMoneyMirrorBook.com/resources

We are what we think. All that we are arises with our thoughts. With our thoughts we make the world

– Buddha

Rae Brent

Resources

To help you avoid potential pitfalls, here are some resources to guide you safely on your journey as you change your reflection in *The Money Mirror*...

If you've enjoyed this book and found it useful, please visit the website for more information on how to change your reflection in *The Money Mirror* at:

www.TheMoneyMirrorBook.com

Or join *The Money Mirror* community at:

www.Facebook.com/TheMoneyMirror/

And if you don't want to write in your book, you can download the complete workbook with all the exercises and tables at:

www.TheMoneyMirrorBook.com/resources

And for a simple and quick way to get your finances under control. I have an online course called "Discipline Your Dollars to Get Out of Debt."

The course is filled with useful tools, tips and resources you can use to change your reflection in *The Money Mirror*.

www.DisciplineYourDollars.com

Rae's Recommended Reading List:

- *Think and Grow Rich* – Napoleon Hill

- *The Richest Man in Babylon* – George S. Clason

- *The Millionaire Mindset* – Gerry Robert

- *The Secret* – Rhonda Byrne

- Anything by Robert Kiyosaki

- *The Science of Success* – Wallace D. Wattles

- *You Were Born Rich* – Bob Proctor

- *Secrets of the Millionaire Mind* – T. Harv Eker

- *Harmonic Wealth* – James Arthur Ray

- *The Alchemist* – Paulo Coelho

About The Author

Rae Brent

Rae Brent, like each and every one of us has been on a journey of self-discovery to find the true secret of wealth. From her modest up brining in Launceston, Tasmania, to joining the Australian Regular Army (ARA) as a young woman, Rae has had a colorful life.

Whilst in the Army, as Rae was working on her own wealth creation strategies, she was guided to help those around her with their financial difficulties. After being medically discharged from the Army in 2005 after 12 years of service, and reaching the rank of Sergeant, Rae began her own journey to discover spirituality. This has inspired Rae to author *The Money Mirror*.

Rae, a Property Investor, Spiritual Entrepreneur, Copywriter and Marketing Strategist, has developed a way to combine *Wealth Creation* with *Spirituality* to allow anyone to reach their highest potential, no matter their spiritual path or their current financial situation.

The two greatest lessons Rae has learned along her journey are:

1.   I am my biggest investment…By investing in myself, I am investing in my future, and

2.   Never let anyone take your dreams away from you – not even you.

As the co-founder of Lifestyle Phoenix Group, Rae is passionate about upholding her company's mission of *"Resurrecting Lifestyle Dreams from Financial Ashes."*

This book certainly gives you the tools to do exactly that, you just need to use them.

And remember, please share this book with your friends and loved ones. Share it with your community and share it on social media.

So, if this book was helpful to you, please leave an honest review on Amazon. You'll be helping others to change their reflection in *The Money Mirror* too.

Thank you.

P.S. Before I sign off. I'd like to invite you to connect with me on Social Media. This way, you can stay up to date with what else I'm working on:

www.Facebook.com/RaeBrent

www.Facebook.com/TheDOGR

www.instagram.com/thedisciplineofgettingrich/

www.ingramcontent.com/pod-product-compliance
Lightning Source LLC
LaVergne TN
LVHW051508080426
835509LV00017B/1986